The Psychophysiology of Everyday Racism and Sexism

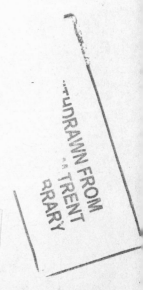

XC

The Psychopathology of Everyday Racism and Sexism

Edited by
Lenora Fulani, PhD

The Psychopathology of Everyday Racism and Sexism, edited by Lenora Fulani, was simultaneously issued by The Haworth Press, Inc., under the title: *The Politics of Race and Gender in Therapy*, a special issue of *Women & Therapy*, Volume 6, Number 4, Winter 1987, Ellen Cole and Esther Rothblum, Editors.

Harrington Park Press
New York • London

ISBN 0-918393-51-5

Published by

Harrington Park Press, Inc., 12 West 32 Street, New York, New York 10001
EUROSPAN/Harrington, 3 Henrietta Street, London WC2E 8LU England

Harrington Park Press, Inc., is a subsidiary of The Haworth Press, Inc., 12 West 32 Street, New
York, New York 10001.

The Psychopathology of Everyday Racism and Sexism was originally published as *Women &
Therapy*, Volume 6, Number 4, Winter 1987.

Cover Design by Marshall Andrews.

LIBRARY OF CONGRESS
Library of Congress Cataloging-in-Publication Data

The Psychopathology of everyday racism and sexism / edited by Lenora Fulani.
    p. cm.
    "Simultaneously issued by the Haworth Press, Inc., under the title: The politics of race and
gender in therapy, a special issue of Women & therapy, volume 6, number 4, winter 1987."
    Includes bibliographies.
    ISBN 0-918393-51-5
    1. Minority women—Mental health—United States. 2. Minority women—United States—
Psychology. 3. Racism—United States—Psychological aspects. 4. Sexism—United States—
Psychological aspects. 5. Psychotherapy—United States. 6. Feminist therapy. I. Fulani, Lenora.
RC451.4.M58P79   1988
305.4'2—dc19   88-6159
                                              CIP

CONTENTS

ABOUT THE EDITOR

Lenora Fulani, PhD, is an internationally known political leader and developmental psychologist. Currently, she is Director of the Community Clinics at the Institute for Social Therapy and Research. Dr. Fulani is Chair of the Women of Color Caucus of the New Alliance Party, and she ran for governor of New York State in 1986 as the only black, the only woman, and the only progressive candidate. With her expertise on issues such as black psychology, multi-racialism, and the gay community, she is in demand as a speaker for federal, state, and local organizations. Dr. Fulani's pioneering work at her Harlem clinic serves as a model for inner city community empowerment.

The Psychopathology of Everyday Racism and Sexism

EDITORIAL

"All Power to the People!" But How?

Lenora Fulani

When I was sixteen years of age one of my older sisters had the first of many mental breakdowns. I often sat with her during these episodes, listening to her angry tirades about herself interspersed with references to racial injustices, sexual abuse, abortions, all

Lenora Fulani, PhD, is an internationally known political leader and developmental psychologist. Currently, she is Director of the Community Clinics at the Institute for Social Therapy and Research. In 1988, Dr. Fulani is an independent candidate for President of the U.S. Dr. Fulani is Chair of the Women of Color Caucus of the New Alliance Party, and ran for governor of New York State in 1986 as the only Black, the only woman, and the only progressive candidate. She is in demand as a speaker for federal, state and local organizations with expertise on issues such as Black psychology, multi-racialism, and the gay community. Dr. Fulani's pioneering work at her Harlem clinic serves as a model for inner-city community empowerment.

mixed together with a deep, deep guilt at her failure as a mother and as a woman. As a sister I sought to reassure her of her self-worth, telling her that she was in no way to blame, that her life had been filled with injustice, that I loved her and had witnessed and shared in the hardship of her life, and that I could personally testify to her strength in overcoming tremendous odds. Sheila, my sister, had gotten pregnant at fifteen, had been married at sixteen and was divorced and alone with two small children by the age of nineteen. She fought her way through all of this, getting a high school degree and a license as a practical nurse and eventually moved her two daughters from the housing project into their own home. It seemed that things were getting better. But my sister never had the opportunity to explore or "work through" the tremendous pain, humiliation and abuse that had been her life, nor deal with the destructive emotional scars that her life and history had left. In many ways gutsy, aggressive and a fighter, my sister was also emotionally quite fragile. Her response and the response of her seventeen year old daughter to the unexpected death of her youngest child produced years of protracted agony, more breakdowns and mental instability, with a great part of both my sister's and her daughter's lives spent in and out of hospital psychiatric wards and mental institutions.

Although my sister's illness had been treated by private doctors, social workers and in various clinics, there had been no improvement or emotional strengthening over the years. The treatment consisted primarily of drugs with little or no attempt to focus on the deeper issues in her life and the life of her family.

This tragedy continues until this day. Moreover, it is, sadly, not exceptional in the emotional lives of women of color. Unfortunately, it is the rule. With but a few changes in the names, places and the shaping of the actual circumstances, you can find my sister in almost any neighborhood in the Black, Latina, Asian and Native American communities across this country. And what you would find would be not only a history of personal tragedy largely due to racism and poverty, but also a history of the failure of traditional psychiatry and psychology to impact on the struggles and problems in the lives of women of color. Traditional mental health treatment has done little but provide a label to emotionally disturbed women, often adding to their hardships with no plan for their cure or empowerment.

I am honored to be the guest editor of a volume on women of color and therapy and eager to share the wealth of experience I and my talented staff have in making an impact on women of color. As the Director of the Community Clinics of the Institute for Social Therapy and Research (ISTR) in New York City, I supervise a multi-racial, gay and straight therapeutic staff that has been developing expertise in the practice of a drug-free, group oriented social therapy, working with Black, Latina, Asian and Native American women, lesbian and straight, poor, working class and middle class. We see white folks, men and children but until recently the clientele at our inner city clinics located in the Bronx and Harlem has predominantly been women of color.

The Community Clinics of the ISTR work with the political/therapeutic perspective (a theory and a practice) that therapy can only be curative, particularly in communities of color, if it is a therapy of *empowerment*. The past 25 years have produced a wealth of experiences in struggles for political and emotional empowerment by and for women of color. Editing this volume has given me the opportunity to reach back and to reach out, to clarify and deepen my own self-consciousness about the therapeutic process and its relation to social change. This has been a challenging and exciting process.

The method of selecting articles for this volume raised the issue of how women of color relate to the institution of therapy. The reality is that we as women of color have an understandably conflicted relationship to that institution. On the one hand, many of our people need psychological help. On the other hand, the function of traditional psychology and psychiatry in American society seems to be adapting people to the society as it is. And the society that patients are being adapted to or assimilated into remains racist, classist, homophobic and sexist to its core. It is a society whose standard of normalcy is *white, middle class, heterosexual and male*. This standard is unachievable for most people in this country and in particular for women of color. There is clearly a profound contradiction when Black, Latina and other women of color are forced to adapt to this society.

Franz Fanon (1967) in *Black Skins, White Masks* spoke extensively of the alienation resulting from oppressed people and, in particular, people of color "being adapted" to a society through the institutions of their oppressor. He describes clearly the alienated Martiniquan who, upon his return from his schooling in Paris where he learns to think, speak and act like a white man, is incapable of further development because he no longer knows or is connected to his culture.

This contradiction, though not often self-consciously understood, is often expressed in the conflicts that women of color share when speaking of their difficulties with therapy and therapists. These conflicts are frequently expressed in racial terms, for example, as a stated preference (or an outright demand!) for a therapist from one's own ethnic group or more often as a concern that an Anglo therapist won't be helpful because of cultural differences. To identify the lack of sensitivity of a therapist as due exclusively to the therapist and not the methodology of traditional treatment is, we believe, wrong. That is not to say that therapists don't vary dramatically in their degrees of sensitivity. But it is very important to recognize that traditional therapy, in its role as a tool of adaptation to normalcy, has built-in biases, limits and constraints which function regardless of the ethnicity, sex, and racial backgrounds of those who use it. What needs to be challenged is not the personalities of the practitioners but the methodology, i.e., the "personality" of the theory and practice they employ.

During the 1960s and early '70s hundreds of thousands of Blacks, Puerto Ricans, Chicanos, women, and lesbians and gay men participated in building mass movements for political liberation. Coming out politically raised a host of complex and painful questions, issues, problems and conflicts, not only for individuals but for the broader political movements to which they were relating. Engaging the emotional, social and cultural conflicts of such a coming out required engaging traditional psychological, social and cultural institutions.

The development of the Black psychology movement of the

1960s was an important attempt to address some of these issues. In many ways it led the way for the women's, lesbian and gay, Latino and community psychology movements, helping to bring to the fore the importance of radicalizing psychology. Black psychology was also a lawful reaction to the structural racism of traditional psychology. It helped to color psychology in that it introduced the notion that one's history—who one is—has relevance to the study of psychology. It also raised the importance of Black history and of consciousness raising. It taught us that we were somebody, that Black folks had a culture, that our problems weren't merely in our heads but that they had a hell of a lot to do with the racist environment in which we lived.

Feminist and lesbian and gay therapies also addressed these fundamental issues about psychology. They raised questions not merely about how traditional therapy was practiced (its obvious sexist and homophobic biases). These new feminist and lesbian and gay therapies brought the therapeutic activity *itself* into question. For example, they raised the question of the relationship between patient and therapist. They raised not only the explicit biases but the male character of the *methodology* in general.

For example, the *authoritarian* nature of the therapist/patient relationship was questioned. What was raised was the question of power and/or authority and who held it in the relationship between patient and therapist—just as the women's and gay movements raised this question with respect to relations between women and men, gay and straight, in the whole of society. In particular, the feminists attempted to build, and to varying degrees succeeded in building, a non-authoritarian model for doing therapy wherein the patient/therapist relationship was not defined by the traditional roles of male/female, dominant/passive, etc., and in which therapist and patient related to each other more as *peers*. It was one of the first times that the legitimacy of the male therapist and male-dominated therapy was brought into question. As a result, many women and many lesbians and gay men were brought into the practice of therapy itself, which impacted profoundly on the whole institution of psychotherapy. Many people who did not have the traditional credentials or licenses were trained, and began practicing. Lay therapists became more socially recognized. It was even discovered that Freud himself (if not his followers) was quite supportive of lay therapists!

Another critical question raised by these new therapies was the question of what the primary therapeutic *unit* was. Previously, it had been assumed to be the *individual*. In the '60s and '70s the *group* became more and more an acceptable unit in the practice of therapy. For some, it became the preferred unit. Third, there was a growing recognition of both the social character and social origins of psychological and emotional problems, a growing recognition that humiliation, victimization and degradation, for example, are not private intra-psychic problems of individuals (although individuals "have them") but rather that these problems are social both in their character *and* in their origins, and thus require a social response — a response by the society as a whole — to resolve them.

But neither Black psychology, feminist and lesbian and gay therapies, nor other forms of radical therapies, in my opinion, went far enough. Their challenge to the role of traditional psychology and psychiatry as tools of social control was limited by their failure to create a fundamentally new form of psychology that not only considered the racial or gender background of the practitioner, or included culturally relevant terms, or broke down the authoritarian therapist/patient relationship, but which challenged the traditional bottom line commitment to adaptation and sought to replace it with a commitment to the empowerment of an entire community through the practice of an empowerment therapy. Radical therapy for the most part stopped far short of this.

Social therapy does not stop short. It is such an empowerment therapy. We are often asked, "If social therapy doesn't adapt people to society, then what does it do?" This is a serious and complex question. Important assumptions concerning the nature of adaptation underlie the question itself. For, while social therapy does not adapt people to society, it does not follow that it is not adaptive. The key question is: Adaptation to what? In order to answer, we have to introduce a distinction that is critical to social therapeutic theory and practice, viz. the distinction between *society* and *history*. Society is, if you will, how history is put together (organized) at a certain moment in a certain location. That is, society is *in* history. Thus, all of us live simultaneously in society (this historically specific organization of history) and in history. One of the features of society is that people are socialized to adapt to *it* — to adapt to society as the-only-thing-in-itself, i.e., ahistorically — and not to history. Indeed, the adaptation to society is sometimes so complete that people do not have an awareness that they *are* in history at all, that history is something it is possible to adapt *to*. Some people call this sociological fact, alienation.

The crises in the social institutions of contemporary society (the family, education, health, politics, religion, etc.) are the result of the increasing inability of people to adapt to a society rapidly destabilizing and, therefore, not only less and less desirable to adapt to but also more and more *difficult* to adapt to. As it becomes harder and harder to adapt people to such a society, more and more coercive measures are employed, e.g., religious Fundamentalism, methadone, etc. Many believe that to adapt people to contemporary society with its many reactionary and fragmented characteristics is itself maladjusted and unethical. To quote Dr. King,

> Today, psychologists have a favorite word, and that word is maladjusted. I tell you today that there are some things in our social system to which I am proud to be maladjusted. I shall never be adjusted to lynch mobs, segregation, economic inequalities, "the madness of militarism," and self-defeating physical violence. The salvation of the world lies in the maladjusted.

I believe there is something we *can* do other than adapting people to society. We can help people adapt to *history*. What does this mean? Broadly speaking, we can help people adapt to history by facilitating the collective experience of building new social environments that meet their emotional needs, rather than adapting impotently and non-developmentally to existing societal environments. The social therapy group is one such new environment. Breaking out of old environments and old roles (which are societally sanctioned) and participating collectively in building new environments (which are historically necessary) is what we mean by "doing empowerment." (See my article in this volume for a deeper discussion of social therapy with poor women of color.)

In putting together this volume, I wanted to find a way to look at psychology, social change and community empowerment, and women of color from both inside and outside the psychological community and discipline. The women who have contributed to this volume share this rich social history (whether or not they themselves were active in these movements), and in different ways their expression carries on the legacy of struggle.

The liberation of women of color gains strong expression through culture. Some of our most passionate voices are Black, Latina, Asian and Native American poets and writers. The selections by Suzana Cabañas, Martha Chabrán, Jessie Fields, Milagros González, Audre Lorde, Sōnia Sanchez, and Judy Simmons are empowered and empowering statements about the conflicts, anger, love, compassion and power of ordinary women. Through these writers (as well as through many of the case studies that appear throughout this volume) ordinary women — mothers, daughters, clients, patients, students — speak out.

An important voice comes from women of color psychologists, those with strong academic training who, like myself, gained access to the university during the '60s and '70s and had to take on its racism and sexism. For a time, we believed we could make it if we became super statisticians and worked twice as hard in order to "overcome our disadvantage" (e.g., our Blackness and our woman-ness). Many of us ultimately broke with this and went on to help develop a psychology that meets *our* needs. The articles by Connie S. Chan, Lillian Comas-Díaz, and Iris Zavala-Martinez are the products of such a history.

The voice of women of color practitioners, too, must be heard. The work they do daily in community clinics, inner city and rural hospitals, schools, community colleges, where people of color are the majority of the clients, is tremendously important, and their closeness to the everyday lives of women of color, especially in their relationship to the family in crisis, gives them a special point of view. The article by Virginia W. Hammond reflects understanding of the subjective issues faced by African American women.

The experience of women of color in the U.S. is more than a

local or regional phenomenon. Our lives are integrally tied to the lives of women of color internationally. We have much to learn from their struggles, failures and successes. Milagros González, a Cuban poet and policewoman, expresses compassionately the objective and subjective experiences of women in dealing with sexism in a society that has eliminated its necessity and is collectively engaged in eliminating its actuality. Nancy Caro Hollander's article about Marie Langer teaches us about emotionality and psychotherapy under conditions of fascism in Argentina, conditions of extreme social control and women's oppression. How are we in the U.S. prepared to empower women of color, not only if fascism comes to the U.S.—but in order to *stop* it from coming?

I have not grown too old or cynical to still be moved by the radical slogan "All Power to the People." I hope I never will. Yet I have learned that empowerment itself must be reorganized in ways that are sensitive to the varied oppression of different peoples as well as to the fundamentality of racism, sexism, classism and homophobia in our social system. To see all this clearly we must find a way to *see* society while *working* in history. To do this, we must empower ourselves. And to do so will take far more than slogans no matter how valid and how moving they may be.

REFERENCES

Fanon, F. (1967). *Black skins, white masks*. New York: Grove Press.
King, M. L., Jr. In S. Oates. (1982). *Let the trumpets sound: The life of Martin Luther King, Jr.* New York: Mentor.

A Song

take my virginity
and convert it to maternity
wait around a century or two
and see what i'll do.

take my body give it yo' brand
stitch my breasts on the fatherland
wait around a decade or two
and see just what i'll do.

place my dreams on any back stair
tune my eyes for yo' nightmare
wait around a century or two
and see what i'll finally do.

suck my breath until i stutter
listen to the sounds i utter
wait around a decade or two
and see just what i'll do.

take my daughter one sunday morn
drape her in dresses to be torn

Soñia Sanchez is the author of twelve books including *Homecoming, We A BaddDDD People, I've Been a Woman: New and Selected Poems*, and most recently, *Homegirls and Handgrenades*. In addition to being a contributing editor to *Black Scholar, Journal of African Studies*, she has edited two anthologies: *We Be Word Sorcerers: 25 Stories by Black Americans*, and *360° of Blackness Coming at You*. A Recipient of a National Endowment of the Arts Award for 1978-79 and the Lucretia Mott Award for 1984, she is a winner of the 1985 American Book Award for her book *Homegirls and Handgrenades*. Soñia Sanchez has lectured at over 500 universities and colleges in the U.S. and has traveled extensively, reading her poetry in Cuba, England, the Caribbean, Australia, the People's Republic of China, and Norway. She is Professor of English at Temple University.

"A Song" appeared in *Homegirls and Handgrenades*. It is reprinted here with the permission of the author and Thunder's Mouth Press, Box 780, New York, NY 10025.

wait around a century or two
and see what i'll finally do.

bury me early all dressed in white
find yourself a brand new wife
wait around a decade or two
and see what she'll finally do.
and see what she'll finally do.

Soñia Sanchez

En la Lucha:
The Economic
and Socioemotional Struggles
of Puerto Rican Women

Iris Zavala-Martinez

INTRODUCTION

Often, when a Puerto Rican woman is asked how she is, how things are going, she will respond with "Pues, ahí, *en la lucha*" ("Well, struggling" or, "in the struggle"). Although I have attempted to discover the origins of this phrase, I have not found any precise information. However, it succinctly epitomizes reality for a large segment of Puerto Rican women. We are struggling, we are in the struggle. This brief phrase in fact summarizes not only historical struggles, but daily struggles to survive, deal with, and overcome a multitude of social, economic, personal, and historical factors which are experienced and reflected by many women's lives. This phrase, therefore, represents a statement about survival, a comment

Dr. Iris Zavala-Martinez is a Puerto Rican clinical psychologist. She was Director of the Hispanic Program of the Worchester Youth Guidance Clinic from 1984 to 1986, and was the Deputy for Mental Health Services for the Executive Office of Human Services for the state of Massachusetts from 1986 to 1987. She has an appointment as Clinical Instructor in Psychology at Cambridge Hospital, Harvard Medical School. Dr. Zavala-Martinez has published numerous articles on mental health and is dedicated to developing the emancipatory potential in therapeutic practice and social action.

This is a revised version of an article published in R. Lefkowitz and A. Withorn (Eds.) *For crying out loud: Women and poverty in the United States.* Pilgrim Press, New York, 1986, pp. 111-124.

3

on economic and social circumstances, a comment on coping and perseverance, and contains seeds of a commitment to be involved, to be engaged, to be in struggle. The popularization of this phrase, almost to the extent of an adage, does not divest it of the broad implications it contains, nor of the historical and social realities it was derived from and refers to.

Puerto Rican women's lives in the United States have been portrayed in limited ways. Often, statistical data are referred to, such as numbers of single heads of households, numbers on welfare, level of educational attainment, percentages obtaining mental health or social services, etc. Such factual data, however, obscure the complexity of Puerto Rican women's lives and do not address the underlying factors which contribute to the statistics. Another portrayal has been that of descriptive comments on functional style, frequently with negative stereotypic undertones. For example, Puerto Rican women have often been stereotyped as passive, submissive, all-suffering women, or as hysterical, loud, and hot tempered. Many Latina and non-Latina women have, in fact, also been portrayed this way. These simplifications distort the lives of Puerto Rican women as such depictions make it seem that Puerto Rican women, for some peculiar or "cultural" reason, are more characteristic of these descriptions than other women regardless of a social and historical context. The function of these descriptions is ideological and certainly adialectical. Similarly, Puerto Rican women are described as if they were all one homogeneous group. Such descriptions foster a myth that ignores the varied typology of Puerto Rican women in the United States. For example, a range of differences can exist involving factors such as class, generation, race, place of birth or rearing, education, language or sexual preference. If we recognize the multitude of interacting differences, we necessarily then question the homogenization of Puerto Rican women as is often depicted in the literature. In this way we can legitimize the dynamic, complex, and changing world of Puerto Rican women.

Less often are we presented with a more specific or in-depth analysis that can do justice to the realities and complexities of the lives of Puerto Rican women in the U.S. This shortcoming, in essence, does not take advantage of the rich interplay of the multiple factors we delineated earlier. It is necessary to note, however, that in the past decade the literature and scholarship on Puerto Rican women by Puerto Ricans has gradually grown and promises to continue doing so. This developing literature has begun to examine critically aspects of the social and historical role of Puerto Rican women, and has begun to, in essence, give voice to her "lucha," to her struggles.

My efforts in this essay are to extend and contribute to that growing body of literature on Puerto Rican women, focusing on the women in the United States. My intent is to summarize the impact of the economic struggles of Puerto Rican women upon their socioemotional life. I will not pretend to analyze the complex economic and political factors involved as this has been done well by others (Center for Puerto Rican Studies, 1979; Centro de Estudios Puertorriqueños, 1976; Maldonado-Denis, 1976). I will, however, make reference to these factors and assume a critical perspective. That is, I will contextualize issues by conceptualizing the interaction of social, economic, and historical factors and how these relate to women's roles and lives; and question and challenge cultural attributes and myths that undermine Puerto Rican women's changing lives. To articulate such a perspective is necessarily to side with the liberating commitment to be "en la lucha." Further, this essay is directed to a vast multi-level collective of sisters, Puerto Rican and non-Puerto Rican, who now seek legitimate sources of study to advance their development. Ultimately, this effort is dedicated to the sisterhood of struggle.

A BRIEF HISTORICAL DETOUR

To understand the struggles of Puerto Rican women in the United States, it is necessary to point out four key social and historical processes that have directly impacted upon Puerto Rican women's reality:

1. The political and economic relationship between Puerto Rico and the United States, i.e., colonialism.
2. The development of capitalism in Puerto Rico and the economic transformation from an agricultural to industrial society.
3. The role and social status of women in Puerto Rico and in a class society.
4. The emerging forms of consciousness and struggle among Puerto Ricans, given the political relationship with the U.S., and among women as part of the women's movement in Puerto Rico, the U.S., and elsewhere.

The impact of capitalism and colonialism on Puerto Ricans, their family dynamics, and ensuing historical effects have been well analyzed by numerous writers (Center for Puerto Rican Studies, 1979; Inclán, 1978; Maldanado-Denis, 1969). Suffice it to say that the systematic development of capitalism in Puerto Rico not only propelled abrupt industrialization, but also ensured economic control of the island as an expanding market and as a source of cheap labor for United States interests. The consequences of these complex socioeconomic processes were to change the fabric of life for the Puerto Rican people.

One such consequence was the massive migrations of Puerto Ricans to the United States in the 1950s and '60s (Center for Puerto Rican Studies, 1979). Another was the incorporation of masses of Puerto Rican women into the labor market in lower-paying and sexually segregated jobs. The proletarianization of women in the first thirty years of this century generated participation in labor struggles and a developing consciousness of sex role relations (Azize, 1979; Rivera Quintero, 1979). In the United States, immigrant Puerto Rican women were increasingly working in piecework as cigarmakers, as domestics, as operatives and unskilled workers, and in service jobs (Korrol, 1980). However, from a labor-force participation of 38.9 percent in 1950, a progressive decline can be observed. The participation of Puerto Rican females in the labor force by 1970 was lower than all other ethnic groups and is attributed to "unfavorable labor-market conditions and large declines in central city industries" (Santana Cooney & Colon, 1980). In New York City, the marked decline in Puerto Rican female labor force participation was inversely related to the increase in female headed households. However, Puerto Rican women in comparison to Puerto Rican men in 1977 had greater labor utilization, a situation which has greatly impacted family and marital relationships (Mizio, 1974; Vasquez, 1979). Immigration and the differential labor participation of women and men generated disruption of family and role conflicts. The traditional role definitions of Puerto Rican men was challenged without there having been available a mechanism to process these abrupt changes. Women struggled to develop themselves in the public sphere of work while maintaining subordinate roles in the home (Christensen, 1979) or attempted to survive independently by resorting to welfare (wilfredo, as some say). The structure of this socioeconomic reality was bound to exert tremendous pressure on the adaptive capacities of anyone.

These experiences are much less cultural — as has often and mistakenly been assumed — than sociohistorical and related to the role of status of women in a society governed by economic interests and patriarchal ideology. In fact, given the way in which Latina and other minority women's lives are often distorted (Andrade, 1982; Zambrana, 1982), it is imperative to adopt a critical and investigative focus on women's changing roles. For example, the salient features of the sociocultural norms for Puerto Rican women are similar to traditional role socialization of many other women. It is perplexing, however, that the literature on Puerto Ricans emphasizes the function of traditional role ascriptions over and above any analysis of interrelated class, historical, economic, or other factors. Further, traditional roles are often seen as the problem for Puerto Rican women rather than the changing reality of class and gender relations resulting from changing socioeconomic and historical forces. This is not to deny, on the other hand, that traditional role ascriptions oppress women's strivings. It is to contextualize this traditionality. As we question the adverse impact of traditional roles and as we come to grips with their anti-feminist functions, we also need to see how these very roles may have mediated stressful life situations. Traditional modes have often been interpreted as counter to modern, more feminist role orientations. Before embracing general feminist prescriptions for modern women's roles, we need to understand those features of traditional roles that helped women to cope with socioeconomic demands and changing historical forces. Puerto Rican women have had to adapt to a multitude of forces and we need to gain an understanding of changing roles in the context of changing sociohistorical forces to appreciate the dialectic between traditional and progressive behaviors in Puerto Rican women. Given this discussion, several questions could be the focus for ongoing scholarship on the lives of Puerto Rican women:

1. To what degree have cultural descriptions obscured the sources of Puerto Rican women's oppression as related to the social relations in a capitalist society?
2. How have Puerto Rican women internalized a false consciousness which attributes their woes to "hombres machistas" (male chauvinists), or to "el destino" (destiny), or to unseen spirits?
3. Why has so much attention been paid to cultural factors and to traditional roles as limitations to Puerto Rican women's development and success?

The fourth historical process to impact on Puerto Rican women is the merging forms of class and feminist consciousness that have characterized the "women's movement" in the United States, in Puerto Rico, and other parts of the world. As women began to examine and analyze the structure of reality and to acquire an understanding into the nature of their oppression, they have had significant influence in promoting certain social changes. Puerto Ricans in the United States have experienced this influence at some level and have engaged in aspects of the feminist experience, whether through community activism, academic scholarship, or personal life. It is crucial to point out that feminism and the women's movement were not imported from the United States or elsewhere. The new analysis of both private life and community activism that defines modern feminism has affected women throughout the world. But feminist liberating consciousness had its own history in Puerto Rico prior to the contemporary women's movement.

To highlight this history and our concept of "en la lucha" it is necessary to pay tribute to the important participation of women in the political and labor struggles of Puerto Rico.

Puerto Rican women have been in the struggle since the days of the Spanish colonizers when Taino women, like the Cacica Yuisa in 1514, for example, resisted their sexual and imperialist advances and were involved individually and as part of a collective resistance against the colonizers. Much less documented is the participation of Black slave women in the hacienda anti-slavery uprisings of the 1800s in Puerto Rico (Baralt, 1982). In the heroic but unsuccessful uprising against the Spaniards in 1868 known as "el Grito de Lares," the name of Marianna Bracetti stands out. She embroidered the Puerto Rican Revolutionary Flag and with other women engaged in different organizing tasks. Another 19th century activist was Lola Rodriguez de Tió, a poetess, whose beliefs in independence twice led to her deportation from Puerto Rico. She is the author of the Puerto Rican national anthem, "La Borinqueña."

It is during this century, however, that more justice has been done to naming and honoring numerous women involved in the political, working class, and feminist struggles of their day. The early suffragettes included educated women such as Ana Roque de Duprey, Mercedes Solá, and Isabel Andreu de Aguilar. These women defended women's rights in writings and through the first feminist organization on the island and represented a middle class current in their feminism. The other current emerges from within the working class and is represented by Concha Torres, the first woman in the island to speak at a political rally; Juana Colón, an organizer of tobacco strippers and a socialist militant; and Luisa Capetillo, whose writings from 1904-1916 became the first feminist manifestos of a new ideology which was anti-patriarchal and in favor of the rights of the working class.

During the 1930s to 1950s, various women became prominent in the nationalist struggles: Blanca Canales, Doris Torresola, and Lolita Lebrón are the best known for their courageous examples and leadership. Puerto Rican women have continued to actively participate in the issues of their day, particularly in the anti-colonialist struggle. Currently a number of Puerto Rican women are political prisoners in U.S. prisons. And to a different degree, Puerto Rican women participate in community and governmental affairs and continue to be part of a long history of struggle. Puerto Rican women, indeed, have been "en la lucha" against colonialism and different forms of oppression for many years (Azize, 1979; Latin American and Caribbean Women's Collective, 1980; Pico, 1979; Zayas & Silen, 1973). To struggle, in fact, is necessary for political, economic and socioemotional survival.

THE STRUCTURE OF REALITY

The current profile of reality reveals the political, economic, and social structure of oppression. The statistical data and the sociohistorical analysis provides an essential background for understanding Puerto Rican women's daily struggle to survive.

According to a 1978 statistical portrait of women in the United States, Puerto Rican women formed 16% of all Hispanic origin women, had a median age of 22.4 years; and among Latin women, had the highest unemployment rate of 12.2%. By 1985, the total Puerto Rican population was 2,562,000 (or 1.1% of the total U.S. population) and 53.2% were women. The median family income for Puerto Ricans overall was $12,371, the *lowest* of all Latino groups and significantly lower than that of non-Latino families of $26,951. In 1985, 41.9% of all Puerto Ricans were living in poverty in comparison to 11.7% for non-Latinos. Only 51% of adult Puerto Ricans were in the labor force in 1985 and the Puerto Rican women labor force participation rate was 39% in comparison to 51% rate among Chicana and Cuban women (Institute for Puerto Rican Policy, 1986; U.S. Bureau of the Census, 1978, 1980).

It is not surprising, therefore, that Puerto Ricans resort to welfare in the United States. The choices are limited as they have been forced to survive through welfare because of high unemployment, low education, and the invisible factors of institutionalized discrimination along with the complex structural reasons related to a colonial economy.

The family constellation has also changed. In 1960, 15.3% of the Puerto Rican families were headed by women; in 1970 this went up to 24.1% and by 1982 this rose to 40% in comparison to white female heads of households of 6% in 1960 and 13.9% in 1982

(Council on Interracial Books for Children, 1984; Santana Cooney & Colón, 1980).

This brief statistical profile indicates that Puerto Ricans are in a very disadvantageous situation particularly in comparison to the white population and other Latino groups. Certainly, such a stark profile has implications for the overall well-being of the Puerto Rican community and for the socioemotional status of women.

THE SOCIOEMOTIONAL PROFILE

The mental health of women has received increased scrutiny over the past fifteen years as an outcome of the women's movement and of the critical re-examination of social and psychological theories. From the mental health literature on women there has emerged some salient findings about women's social roles and their emotional status. The experience of women as housewives and mothers has been found to be stressful and associated with emotional difficulties (Gove & Tudor, 1973; Weissman & Klerman, 1977), whereas depression in working class woman has been associated with socioeconomic factors (Brown & Harris 1978). Lack of power over one's life has been associated with psychological problems (Dohrenwend, 1973) and low social status and powerlessness are seen as making people more vulnerable to emotional stress (Al-Issa, 1980). Further, environmental factors have been found to adversely affect lower class women's physical and mental health (Duvall & Booth, 1978). In summary, these findings suggest that women whose lives are characterized by these factors are at risk of a distressing socioemotional reality.

Our discussion of the structure of reality indicated that Puerto Rican women are in a disadvantageous economic situation, are increasingly single heads of households, are not well represented in the labor force, live in poor communities, and consequently have fewer opportunities for self-realization and power. The effects of all forms of inequality on women's mental health in general have been well documented (Carmen, Russo & Miller, 1981) and other literature has highlighted the impact of discrimination, migration, and cultural conflict upon an individual's mental health. Given all of this, what does the mental health profile of Puerto Rican women in the U.S. look like?

First, it is important to point out that some of the data available at best can only provide tentative information, as epidemiological data sources on Puerto Rican women are often subsumed within general statistics on Puerto Rican mental health and the methodology and conceptual underpinnings of these findings have been questioned (Zavala-Martinez, 1981). Second, it is crucial to delineate all the factors which impact on the mental health of Puerto Rican women, along with those economic and social factors identified for women in general.

Comas-Diaz (1982) reported that Puerto Rican women are exposed to various stressors that impact on their mental health: different forms of discrimination, cultural role expectations, and acculturation factors. To this list, and underlying these stressors, are the adverse consequences of poverty, family disruption, language limitation, and lack of meaningful employment. Of particular importance is the tension created for Puerto Rican women between learned role behaviors that correspond to a traditional view of women, and the needs, potential, and strivings which are in conflict with these cultural role expectations. The sociocultural and historical trend has been that women are self-sacrificing wives and mothers, subordinate to men, and therefore in a powerless, helpless position. They are expected to accept this "reality" and not to demonstrate anger, aggressivity, nor independent functioning. It is crucial to understand that Puerto Rican women's experiences reflect the internalization of historical and social forces that were mentioned earlier: the impact of colonialism and patriarchal ideology. Colonization is an oppressive economic, political, and social situation which is internalized through psychological dynamics that are mediated and legitimized by the prevailing social institutions (Zavala-Martinez, 1981). Puerto Rican women not only develop and internalize an ideology of dependency and subjugation based on the historical-political relationships of Puerto Rico, but also experience the social affirmation and perpetuation of this ideology through the dictates of patriarchy as legitimized by Catholicism and the culture of familism. Though these assertions need further elaboration we can only make reference to them here. Taken together, these forces strongly militate against Puerto Rican women's struggle for self-determination, autonomy, and optimal development and well-being.

Indeed, Puerto Rican women experience two forms of oppression, two forms of colonialism (Urdang, 1979). They are oppressed by the external dominant system and by their own socialization process and cultural expectations. Miranda (1979) describes the situation of the Puerto Rican woman in the United States and clearly delineates the "impact of double discrimination." Accordingly, the Puerto Rican woman is "entrapped within the bleak economic and political powerlessness affecting the Puerto Rican population in general. . . . On the other hand, she suffers from the socialization of sex roles that cause her to have guilt feelings about the fulfillment of her potential." This tension and eventual conflict often get manifested in various forms of psychological symptomatology. Soto and Shaver (1982) examined the relationship between some of the factors that have been identified, namely role traditionality, assertiveness, and psychological symptoms in a sample of Puerto Rican women in New York. Indeed, women who were more traditional were less assertive and tended to be less educated and first generation U.S. residents. Less assertive women, in turn, had greater indices of psychological symptoms such as depression and somatization. Similar findings were earlier obtained by Torres Matrullo (1976) in that greater symptomatology was observed in more traditional women. Inclán (1983) examined symptomatology among second generation Puerto Rican women of different socioeconomic groupings and found that low socioeconomic status was directly associated with higher reports of symptomatology. The impact of adverse environmental and socioeconomic factors was confirmed in a study by Zavala-Martinez (1980). She found that women who were poor, who had had lesser educational opportunities, and lived in dire housing situations reported high rates of frustration, depression, and somatic complaints. Clinical reports on Puerto Rican women's mental health have noted the high incidence of depression, somatization, "nervios" (nerves), anxiety, along with feelings of powerlessness, fear of losing control, inadequacy, negative self-appraisal and frustrations (no valgo, estoy agobida, aborrecida) (Abad & Boyce, 1979; Comas-Diaz, 1982). "Nervios" and "ataque" are socioculturally syntonic heightened stress manifestations that have been reported in Puerto Rican men and women which appear to epitomize the dialectics of anger and powerlessness (Zavala-Martinez, in preparation).

This brief summary has attempted to provide a socioemotional profile that can do justice to Puerto Rican women's reality. It suffices to note that Puerto Rican women's mental health is at risk given the multiplicity and complexity of interacting factors that characterize her overall situation. The important questions, therefore, are: How have women coped? What have they done to overcome the socioemotional impact of socioeconomic inequities? How have they persevered? Before we examine the survival strategies and their socioemotional role in helping Puerto Ricans to cope, I will need to review some life histories.

LIFE HISTORIES

This discussion can be energized by providing real life examples of Puerto Rican women's socioemotional struggles. These cases (names were changed) represent women actually seen in my public therapy practice and reveal the impact of the interacting forces we have delineated upon Puerto Rican women's mental health. It must be clarified that an important dimension of psychological functioning has not been elaborated upon here, i.e., the adverse impact of past childhood experiences. This dimension is recognized as important and sometimes crucial, although it is not wholly elaborated here. Further, these brief case histories reflect one end of the continuum of possible mental health cases as they better illustrate our points.

Carmen was a 19 year old working class woman who came to the United States to live with an aunt, for a change of environment (cambiar de ambiente) and in hopes of learning to "do something," to earn a living and support herself. She was fleeing a very strict father who entrusted her to his sister. Carmen was ambitious and very idealistic. She began English classes and enrolled in a vocational training program in the Latino community. Nine months after her arrival she had gained some ability to communicate in English and would laughingly and self-consciously show off her newly acquired skill.

At this time her aunt became quite ill and Carmen had to quit some of her activities and care for her. Although the aunt had teenage children who had been raised in the U.S. and who spoke English, they felt less obligation than Carmen to look after her. Carmen felt obliged as she depended on her aunt for housing and because she felt indebted to her for taking her in and providing her with a refuge from an authoritarian father. She also felt that it was "expected" of her to take care of her aunt without complaining, without uttering a word of discomfort.

Two months later Carmen came into an out-patient mental health clinic complaining of tension headaches, of feelings of wanting to yell and throw things, and of sudden crying spells. She made self-deprecatory remarks about how she was selfish, how she would not amount to anything in life, how she had no real skills, and how she was not intelligent.

María was a divorced woman with three children who had been in the U.S. for ten years. Her husband had been gone for three years, and she had been struggling to make ends meet and to raise her children. She knew enough English to "defenderse," or "get along," but she had limited vocational skills and could only find work in a shoe factory. She worked from 8:30 a.m. until 4:30 p.m. but her children got out of school at 2:30 p.m., which meant that they were alone in the afternoon, supervised by her eldest child, an 11 year old. María did not make enough money to pay for a child caretaker, and she had not developed a support system after her husband left.

The sexualized overtones of comments from a fellow worker had made her feel increasingly anxious and at home she had become overwhelmed and tense about household demands. She had been getting increasingly irritated with her children, scolding them more and more often. She had not been sleeping well for a while and was seeking something to calm her nerves. She resorted to a "traguito," a drink which often was a beer or two. The children had become increasingly hard to control and María was losing her control. When the oldest boy disappeared for over five hours one afternoon, María became quite agitated, guilt ridden, lost control, and experienced an "ataque de nervios," a heightened acute stress reaction whereby she fell to the floor while flaying her hands and sobbing uncontrollably. A neighbor came to her assistance and brought a very distraught María to a clinic.

Ana was a 28 year old woman who had been raised in the U.S. since she was three years old. For two and half years she had been married to an island-born Puerto Rican, Ernesto, who had been in the U.S. for the past five years. For over six months she and her husband had been increasingly fighting and often Ernesto would storm out of the house and not return for hours. Ana's family lived in New York while her husband's family lived in Puerto Rico. Ernesto felt very little support for himself, was antagonistic to the "Americanos," had difficulty holding a job, and spoke little English. He felt angry all the time and didn't know why. He also felt displaced and alone.

Ana had studied and was a medical assistant in an area hospital. As she was bilingual, her skills were in demand and she felt good about working. Ernesto constantly berated Ana and was critical of any of her activities or of her way of dressing. Often he was verbally and emotionally abusive. Ana had become overwhelmed by his attitudes and has begun to doubt herself and her choice of spouse. She also had become increasingly depressed and withdrawn. While suppressing intense anger at her husband, she felt helpless and very stressed out.

All three women described here have been exposed to the general stresses upon women that were mentioned earlier. In addition, they face particular problems as Puerto Rican women. They encounter different forms of discrimination—ethnic, class, gender and race—in work and community life. They face the psychosocial pressures of immigration, such as loss of homeland and dislocation. They must deal with mastery of the English language, issues of cultural identity and other stresses associated with cultural adaptation and value conflicts. And they are subject to the particular sex role expectations of their culture while attempting to define and to develop themselves. The interaction of these factors can tax the coping ability of any woman, as it did in the cases of Carmen, María and Ana, and result in psychological stress reactions.

These cases document the tensions we reviewed earlier; they highlight the struggle against different forms of oppressive experiences, and they epitomize the relationships between broader social and historical forces and individual functioning. But women's conflict is often precipitated when they encounter the cumulative injustices of their situation, are not prepared to handle the excessive demands, and feel powerless to effect change. In the words of Urdang (1979), "the key to the perpetuation of such oppression is in the ability of the oppressor to persuade the oppressed to cooperate in their servitude." Carmen, María, and Ana could not be persuaded, at risk of diminished emotional well-being and of precipitating symptomatology.

Now we need to interpret these life histories according to the earlier review of the mental health literature of women, to the structure of their realities, and to the sociohistorical and cultural forces they are part of.

Carmen can be seen as a young woman trying to develop herself within the limits and possibilities of cultural family expectations. She has turned against herself in conflict over her own strivings. Her attempts are frustrated by social demands and she is angry, but she cannot show her anger, lest she be seen as "ingrata" or ungrateful by her aunt. She must suppress her anger, and her strivings for autonomy and self-improvement. The conflict between these strivings and the expectations she perceives, lead to heightened distress, depression, and difficulty in negotiating change within her family context.

María presents the struggle of a woman attempting to survive without a support system and whose work needs create stress and guilt about her mothering responsibilities. She had attempted to provide for her children emotionally and economically, and she had attempted to take on too much by herself to compensate for her husband's absence. In many ways she had internalized certain aspects of "hembrismo," a sociocultural notion that sustains an ideal of women as strong, persevering, self-sufficient. It's a notion akin to that of "supermadre" (Chaney, 1979) or super-mom which is a very unrealistic ideal for lower-class working women as it sets up unfair expectations.

As María struggled to provide for her children and to assume two parenting roles, she was conflicted by the extreme demands of the outside world as well as those she placed on herself as a proud woman. Although María had lived for some years in the United States, she had not developed a support system, a community of solidarity. Her family was unavailable and she had withdrawn herself from social contact. She feared failure, resorting to AFDC, and not being able to meet the needs of her children. She did not even allow herself any recognition of her own needs, particularly her sexual needs which created tremendous anxiety for her.

María had experienced both sexual and class discrimination and had ignored their psychological effects on her. She had been so intent on providing economically for her children that she had neglected their emotional needs and hers, becoming easily irritated and guilt-ridden. To alleviate her mounting stress she had begun to drink alcohol before going to bed. Plagued by feelings of inadequacy, by fears of failure, fears of not being educated enough to seek help, she had circumscribed her world to work and home, instead of seeing how forces outside her world affected her options and, in fact, structured her psychological responses.

In addition to similarities with Carmen and María, *Ana* reflects the conflict of "success." Her achievement of biculturality, economic status and autonomy came at the expense of confusion and marital strife. At the same time, Ernesto is an example of the privatized reactions to economic displacement experienced by minority men. Neither Ernesto nor Ana can see the social context of their marital strife, nor how different cultural and educational experiences underlie their disagreements. They personalize a conflict that is rooted in the reality of differential experiences, of economic injustice, of colonialist history—a conflict which represents, in some ways, the struggle of a divided nation.

These examples reveal that life for working-class Puerto Rican women is a vulnerable one. I again reiterate some key questions:

How have women coped? What have they done to overcome adversities, attitudinal limitations and structural barriers?

COPING AND SURVIVING

The unifying theme of the history, social status and psychological processes mentioned above is that, through them all, Puerto Rican women are struggling to survive. The examples of the Taina, the slave, the revolutionaries and the militants provide a rich heritage to continue. In addition, contemporary Puerto Rican women have internalized ways of resistance, some passive, some active, with which to survive. These can be counterposed to some of the more self-defeating patterns that can result in symptomatology, but which paradoxically can also provide a pathway to developing better coping skills and a better sense of self.

Puerto Rican women have mastered many "passive" methods of coping. For example, a common adage states that women know how to "salirse con la suya," or get "what they want." The implication is that by using unassuming, indirect, passive or covert methods, a Puerto Rican woman can get what she needs and wants. The value placed on this ability implies that a direct approach would not be successful. Thus, within existing social norms, some Puerto Rican women may learn manipulative approaches to counter oppressive familial and male attitudes and situations (Lopez-Garriga, 1978). These covert approaches respond to and emerge from a context where assertiveness and direct expressions are not allowed or valued and have been used by oppressed peoples everywhere. It has also been said that Puerto Ricans have a tendency to avoid direct expressions and confrontations, and to deny hostile thoughts and feelings. Given Puerto Rico's history of domination by an outside force, these manifestations emerge as learned survival tactics. Although these attempts at covert control can be adaptive and successful, the inability to find open methods of assertion and expression can be detrimental to psychological well-being. The price paid for accumulated emotions seeking an outlet is often somatic complaints, or in an "ataque," or another symptomatic manifestation of distress. Coping attempts like these can extort a high personal price.

They are privatized individual efforts to deal with forces rooted elsewhere.

Puerto Rican women have also used more active, socially sanctioned, strategies to seek self-esteem, survive, obtain power and promote change. Education, for example, has been a means by which individual women have tried to improve their chances of coping and surviving. Given all the forces working against her, if a Puerto Rican woman can become educated she is more employable, more economically independent and more able to participate as a competent autonomous individual in the community and not as the extension of a man or of her children. Carmen, for example, was especially frustrated because her educational route to self-actualization and independency was thwarted by her aunt's illness.

"Hembrismo" is another overt way to cope. Through it, a woman adheres to the cultural script of motherhood, but by being exceptionally strong and powerful in linking various roles she gains power and recognition. This strategy can give a determined woman a certain adaptive strength, although it can also establish ideals that conflict with her own development and strivings. As we saw with Maria, when the objective pressures increase, the very strategy which gave strength in the past can become a barrier to flexibility and problem solving.

The kinship system is most often identified as the source of support for Puerto Rican women. It can often be a first resort in times of trouble without which a woman's life is harder — as we saw with Ana. But the expectations of kin — both real and assumed — can also be a source of stress, as Carmen's distress shows.

For Puerto Rican women, the reliance on the extended family is culturally encouraged and often socioeconomically necessary. But extended family systems have their particular dialectics and go through their own growth and conflicts and are not always the best support. In the U.S. kin may not be close by. While for some this may create a sense of isolation and loss, for others their absence may motivate development of non-kin support networks such as folk healers, religious groups, neighborhood and community groups — which may benefit women who are single parents or are experiencing serious emotional difficulties (Garrison, 1978; Vasquez Nuttall, 1979).

Many of the increasing numbers of Puerto Rican women who are heads of their households have learned the mixed blessing of welfare as a coping strategy. While financial public assistance can provide women with the chance to become somewhat independent of family or men, that "freedom" may be illusive. It forces women to go against the dominant and respected values of the culture without really providing economic autonomy in return. In fact, welfare structures dependency while appearing to provide economic viability. The female headed family, it turns out, is not at all a cultural phenomenon, but a "functional adaptation to a specific economic situation; a situation which leaves the lower class male unable to provide long term maintenance for a family" (Morris, 1979). Many Puerto Rican women therefore have little choice but to resort to public resources, and to develop their own resources and networks of support in order to survive.

More recently, different types of groups of Puerto Rican women have developed in some communities (personal communication). These may be therapeutic and attempt to cope with their personal and emotional needs, and they may be action oriented to provide an organizing base for community change. When women come together to discuss anything from feelings of depression, to issues of parenting, to conducting a rent strike, they transform passive, self-defeating responses into an active participatory way of dealing with their personal difficulties, their social concerns, and their educational and political needs. In such a group Carmen, María, and Ana could begin to talk with others about problems, opportunities and ways to make change. Sometimes individual or family intervention is needed to ameliorate a highly dysfunctional situation (Canino, 1982) and sometimes a woman will not feel comfortable in a group. Should this be the case, therapy's role would be to provide a mode of interaction and dialogue, and a way of understanding socioemotional difficulties towards developing ways of gaining control over adversity, towards overcoming feelings of powerlessness, frustration, and poor self-esteem. The practitioner/therapist needs to engage in helping women regain a sense of self-hood that is often fragmented, privatized, and dissociated from its embeddedness in a social structure (Zavala-Martinez, 1985).

Such encounters could provide a forum for transforming privatized emotional experiences into a collective process of healing. They could provide a way for Puerto Rican women to resist the fragmentation of our people whether by place of birth, skin color, dominant language, gender, or clan. They could help women discover new ways of negotiating change with or without a "professional helper" depending upon the severity of the psychological issues. In summary, this coming together of women continues to legitimize an important Puerto Rican tradition: to struggle, to survive, to be "en la lucha" as a statement of affirmation and perseverance.

REFERENCES

Abad, V. and Boyce, E. (1979). Issues in psychiatric evaluations of Puerto Ricans: A socio-cultural perspective. *Journal of Operational Psychiatry*, 10(1), 28-39.

Al-Issa, I. (1980). *The psychopathology of women*. Englewood Cliffs: Prentice Hall.

Adrade, S. (1982). Family roles of Hispanic women: Stereotypes, empirical findings, and implications for research. In R. Zambrana (Ed.), *Work, family and health: Latino women in transition*. New York: Hispanic Research Center.

Azize, Y. (1979). *Luchas de la mujer en Puerto Rico, 1898-1919*. Puerto Rico: Litografia Metropolitana.

Baralt, G. (1982). *Esclavos rebeldes: Conspiraciones y sublevaciones de escalvos en Puerto Rico (1795-1873)*. Rio Piedras: Endiciones Huracán.

Brown, G. and Harris, T. (1978). *Social origins of depression: A study of psychiatric disorder in women*. New York: Free Press.

Canino, G. (1982). The Hispanic woman: Sociocultural influences on diagnoses and treatment. In R. M. Becerra, M. Karno, and J. Escobar, *Mental health and Hispanic Americans: Clinical perspectives* (pp. 117-138). New York: Grune and Stratton.

Carmen, E., Russo, N., & Miller, J. (1981). Inequality and women's mental health: An overview. *American Journal of Psychiatry*, 138(10), 1319-1330.

Casaus, L., & Andrade, S. (1983). A description of Latinos in the United States: Demographic and sociocultural factors of the past and the future. In S. Andrade (Ed.), *Latino families in the United States*. Planned Parenthood Federation of America, 17.

Center for Puerto Rican Studies (1979). *Labor migration under capitalism: The Puerto Rican experience*. New York: Monthly Review Press.

Centro de Estudios Puertorrigueños (1976). *Los Puertorrigueños y la cultura: Critica y debate conferencia de historiografia, 1974*. New York: Research Foundation, CUNY.

Chaney, E. (1979). *Supermadre: Women in politics in Latin America*. Austin: Univ. of Texas Press.

Christensen, E. (1979). The Puerto Rican woman: A profile. In E. Acosta-Belen (Ed.), *The Puerto-Rican woman*. New York: Praeger.

Comas-Diaz, L. (1982). Mental health needs of Puerto Rican women in the United States. In R. Zambrana (Ed.), *Work, family and health: Latina women in transition*. New York: Hispanic Research Center.

Council of Interracial Books for Children (1984). *Fact Sheets on Institutional Racism*, Nov. 1984, 7.

Dohrenwend, B. (1973). Social status of stressful life events. *Journal of Personality and Social Psychology, 28*, 225-235.

Duvall, D., & Booth, A. (1978). The housing environment and women's health. *Journal of Health and Social Behavior, 19*(4), 410-417.

Garrison, V. (1978). Support systems of schizophrenic and nonschizophrenic Puerto Rican migrant women in New York City. *Schizophrenia Bulletin, 4*(4), 561-595.

Gove, W., & Tudor, J. (1973). Adult sex roles and mental illness. *American Journal of Sociology, 78*, 812-835.

Inclán, J. (1978). *Socioeconomic changes in Puerto Rico: The development of the modern proletarian family*. Unpublished paper.

Inclán, J. (1983). Psychological symptomatology in second generation Puerto Rican women of three socioeconomic groups. *Journal of Community Psychology, 11*, 334-345.

Institute for Puerto Rican Policy (1986). On the Puerto Rican community: Findings from the March, 1985 current population survey. *Datanote, 4, March*.

Latin American and Caribbean Women's Collective (1980). Puerto Rico: Women, culture and colonialism. In *Slave of slaves: The challenge of Latin American women* (pp. 132-146). London: ZED Press.

Lopez-Garriga, M. (1978). Estratégias de autoafirmación en mujeres Puertorriqueñas, *Revista de Ciencias Sociales, 20*(3-4), 257-285.

Maldonado-Denis, M. (1969). *Puerto Rico: Una interpretacion historico-social*. Mexico: Siglo Veintiuno.

Maldonado-Denis, M. (1976). *Puerto Rico y Estados Unidos: Emigración y colonialismo*. Mexico: Siglo Veintiuno.

Miranda, L. (1979). Puertorriqueñas in the United States: The impact of double discrimination. In E. Acosta-Belen (Ed.), *The Puerto Rican woman* (pp. 124-133). New York: Praeger.

Mizio, E. (1974). Impact of external systems on the Puerto Rican family. *Social Casework, 55*(2), 76-89.

Morris, L. (1979). Women without men: Domestic organizations and the welfare state as seen in a coastal community of Puerto Rico. *British Journal of Sociology, 30*(3), 322-40.

Pico, I. (1980). The history of women's struggle for equality in Puerto Rico. In E. Acosta-Belen (Ed.), *The Puerto Rican woman*. New York: Praeger.

Rivera Quintero, M. (1979). The development of capitalism in Puerto Rico and the incorporation of women into the labor force. In E. Acosta-Belen (Ed.), *The Puerto-Rican woman*. New York: Praeger.

Santana Cooney, R., & Colón, A. (1980). Work and family: The recent struggle of Puerto Rican females. In C. Rodríguez, V. Sanchez Karrol, & J. O. Alers (Eds.), *The Puerto Rican struggle: Essays on survival in the United States* (pp. 65-66). New York: Puerto Rican Migration Research Consortium, Inc.

Sánchez Korrol, V. (1980). Survival of Puerto Rican women in New York before World War II. In C. Rodriguez, V. Sanchez Korrol, and J. O. Alers (Eds.), *The Puerto Rican struggle: Essays on survival in the United States*. New York: Puerto Rican Migration Research Consortium, Inc.

Soto, E., & Shaver, P. (1982). Sex-role traditionalism, assertiveness, and symptoms of Puerto Rican women living in the United States. *Hispanic Journal of Behavioral Sciences, 4*(1), 1-20.

Torres-Matrullo, C. (1979). Acculturation and psychopathology among Puerto Rican women in mainland United States. *American Journal of Orthopsychiatry, 46*(4), 710-719.

U.S. Bureau of the Census (1980). *A statistical portrait of women in the United States: 1978* (Current Population Reports, Special Studies, Series P-23, No. 100). Washington, D.C.: U.S. Government Printing Office.

Urdang, S. (1979). *Fighting two colonialisms: Women in Guinea-Bissau* (pp. 12-17). New York: Monthly Review Press.

Vazquez, M. (1979). The effects of role expectations on the marital status of urban Puerto Rican women. In E. Acosta-Belen (Ed.), *The Puerto Rican woman*. New York: Praeger.

Vasquez Nuttall, E. (1979). The support system and coping patterns of the female Puerto Rican single parent. *Journal of Non-white Concerns, 7*(3), 128-37.

Weissman, M., & Klerman, L. (1977). Sex differences and the epidemiology of depression. *Archives of General Psychiatry, 34*, 98-111.

Zambrana, R. (1982). Introduction. In R. Zambrana (Ed.), *Work, family, and health: Latina women in transition*. New York: Hispanic Research Center.

Zavala-Martinez, I. *The dialectics of ataque and colonialism: towards a critical re-examination*. Manuscript in preparation for publication.

Zavala-Martinez, I. (1980). *Identifying mental health needs in an Hispanic community: Towards a participatory methodology*. Unpublished Manuscript, University of Massachusetts, Masters Thesis Collection.

Zavala-Martinez, I. (1981). Puerto Ricans and mental health: An overview of research and clinical data. In *Mental health and the Puerto Ricans in the United States: A critical literature review*. Unpublished manuscript. Available from the author or the Center for Puerto Rican Studies, Hunter College, New York.

Zavala-Martinez, I. (1985). Toward an emancipatory clinical practice in human services. In David and Eva Gil (Eds.), *Toward social and economic justice* (pp. 55-62). Cambridge, Massachusetts: Schenkman Pub. Co.

Zayas, N., & Silen, J. (1973). *La mujer en la lucha hoy*. Rio Piedras: Zayas and Silen.

I Am Your Sister:
Black Women Organizing
Across Sexualities

Audre Lorde

Whenever I come to Medgar Evers College I always feel a thrill of anticipation and delight because it feels like coming home, like talking to family, having a chance to speak about things that are very important to me with people who matter the most. And this is particularly true whenever I talk at the Women's Center. But, as with all families, we sometimes find it difficult to deal constructively with the genuine differences between us and to recognize that unity does not require that we be identical to each other. Black women are not one great vat of homogenized chocolate milk. We have many different faces, and we do not have to become each other in order to work together.

It is not easy for me to speak here with you as a Black Lesbian feminist recognizing that some of the ways in which I identify myself make it difficult for you to hear me. But meeting across difference always requires mutual stretching and until you *can* hear me as a Black Lesbian feminist, our strengths will not be truly available to each other as Black women.

Because I feel it is urgent that we not waste each other's re-

Audre Lorde is a Black woman, lesbian, feminist, mother of two children, daughter of Grenadian immigrants, educator, cancer survivor, activist. Her most recent book is a collection of poetry entitled, *Our Dead Behind Us*, and her forthcoming book, due in 1988, is a collection of essays, *A Burst of Light*.

"I Am Your Sister: Black Women Organizing Across Sexualities" is #3 in the Freedom Organizing Pamphlet Series, published by Kitchen Table: Women of Color Press, P.O. Box 2753, New York, NY 10185. It is reprinted here with the permission of the author and Kitchen Table: Women of Color Press.

25

sources, that we recognize each sister on her own terms so that we may better work together toward our mutual survival, I speak here about heterosexism and homophobia, two grave barriers to organizing among Black women. And so that we have a common language between us, I would like to define some of the terms I use. HETEROSEXISM: A belief in the inherent superiority of one form of loving over all others and thereby the right to dominance. HOMOPHOBIA: A terror surrounding feelings of love for members of the same sex and thereby a hatred of those feelings in others.

In the 1960s, when liberal white people decided that they didn't want to appear racist, they wore dashikis, and danced Black, and ate Black, and even married Black, but they did not want to feel Black or even think Black, so they never even questioned the textures of their daily living (why should flesh-colored bandaids always be pink) and then they always wondered "why are those Black folks always taking offense so easily at the least little thing? Some of our best friends are Black. . . ."

Well, it is not necessary for some of your best friends to be Lesbian, although some of them probably are, no doubt. But it is necessary for you to stop oppressing me through false judgement. I do not want you to ignore my identity, nor do I want you to make it an insurmountable barrier between our sharing of strengths.

When I say I am a Black feminist, I mean I recognize that my power as well as my primary oppressions come as a result of my Blackness as well as my womanness, and therefore my struggles on both these fronts are inseparable.

When I say I am a Black Lesbian, I mean I am a woman whose primary focus of loving, physical as well as emotional, is directed to women. It does not mean I hate men. Far from it. The harshest attacks I have ever heard against Black men come from those women who are intimately bound to them and cannot free themselves from a subservient and silent position. I would never presume to speak about Black men the way I have heard some of my straight sisters talk about the men they are attached to. And of course that concerns me, because it reflects a situation of non-communication in the heterosexual Black community that is far more truly threatening than the existence of Black Lesbians.

What does this have to do with Black women organizing?

I have heard it said—usually behind my back—that Black Lesbians are not normal. But what is normal in this deranged society by which we are all trapped? I remember, and so do many of you, when being Black was considered NOT NORMAL, when they talked about us in whispers, tried to paint us, lynch us, bleach us, ignore us, pretend we did not exist. We called that racism.

I have heard it said that Black Lesbians are a threat to the Black family. But when 50% of children born to Black women are born out of wedlock, and 30% of all Black families are headed by women without husbands, we need to broaden and redefine what we mean by family.

I have heard it said that Black Lesbians will mean the death of the race. Yet Black Lesbians bear children in exactly the same way other women bear children, and a Lesbian household is simply another kind of family. Ask my son and daughter.

The terror of Black Lesbians is buried in that deep inner place where we have been taught to fear all difference — to kill it or ignore it. Be assured — loving women is not a communicable disease. You don't catch it like the common cold. Yet the one accusation that seems to render even the most vocal straight Black woman totally silent and ineffective is the suggestion that she might be a Black Lesbian.

If someone says you're Russian and you know you're not, you don't collapse into stunned silence. Even if someone calls you a bigamist, or a childbeater, and you know you're not, you don't crumple into bits. You say it's not true, and keep on printing the posters. But let anyone, particularly a Black man, accuse a straight Black woman of being a Black Lesbian, and right away that sister becomes immobilized, as if that is the most horrible thing she could be, and must at all costs be proven false. That is homophobia. It is a waste of woman energy, and it puts a terrible weapon into the hands of your enemies to be used against you to silence you, to keep you docile and in line. It also serves to keep us isolated and apart.

I have heard it said that Black Lesbians are not political, that we have not been and are not involved in the struggles of Black people. But when I taught Black and Puerto Rican students writing at City College in the SEEK program in the '60s I was a Black Lesbian. I was a Black Lesbian when I helped organize and fight for the Black Studies Department of John Jay College. And because I was 15 years younger then and less sure of myself, at one crucial moment I yielded to pressures that said I should step back for a Black man even though I knew him to be a serious error of choice, and I did, and he was. But I was a Black Lesbian then.

When my girl friends and I went out in the car one July 4th night after fireworks with cans of white spray paint and our kids asleep in the back of the car, one of us staying behind to keep the motor running and watch the kids while the other two worked our way down the suburban New Jersey street, spraying white paint over the black jockey statues and their little red jackets too, we were Lesbians.

When I drove through the Mississippi delta to Jackson in 1968 with a group of Black students from Tougaloo, another car full of redneck kids trying to bump us off the road all the way back into town, I was a Black Lesbian.

When I weaned my daughter in 1963 to go to Washington in August to work in the coffee tents along with Lena Horne, making coffee for the marshals because that was what most Black women did in the 1963 March on Washington, I was a Black Lesbian.

When I taught a poetry workshop at Tougaloo, a small Black college in Mississippi, where white rowdies shot up the edge of campus every night, and I felt the joy of seeing young Black poets find their voices and power through words in our mutual growth, I was a Black Lesbian. And there are strong Black poets today who date their growth and awareness from those workshops.

When Yoli and I cooked curried chicken and beans and rice and took our extra blankets and pillows up the hill to the striking students occupying buildings at City College in 1969, demanding open admissions and the right to an education, I was a Black Lesbian. When I walked through the midnight hallways of Lehman College that same year, carrying Midol and Kotex pads for the young Black radical women taking part in the action, and we tried to persuade them that their place in the revolution was not ten paces behind Black men, that spreading their legs to the guys on the tables in the cafeteria was not a revolutionary act no matter what the brothers said, I was a Black Lesbian. When I picketed for Welfare Mother's Rights, and against the enforced sterilization of young Black girls, when I fought institutionalized racism in the New York City schools, I was a Black Lesbian.

But you did not know it, because we did not identify ourselves, so now you can still say that Black Lesbians and gay men have nothing to do with the struggles of the Black Nation.

And I am not alone.

When you read the words of Langston Hughes you are reading the words of a Black gay man. When you read the words of Alice Dunbar-Nelson and Angelina Weld Grimke, poets of the Harlem Renaissance, you are reading the words of Black Lesbians. When you listen to the life-affirming voice of Bessie Smith and Ma Rainey, you are hearing Black Lesbian women. When you see the plays and read the words of Lorraine Hansberry, you are reading the words of a woman who loved women deeply.

Today, some of the most active and engaged members of "Art Against Apartheid" which is making visible and immediate our cultural responsibilities against the tragedy of South Africa are Lesbians and gay men. We have organizations such as the National Coalition of Black Lesbians and Gays, Dykes Against Racism Everywhere, and Men of All Colors Together, all of whom are committed to and engaged in anti-racist activity.

Homophobia and heterosexism mean you allow yourselves to be robbed of the sisterhood and strength of Black Lesbian women because you are afraid of being called a Lesbian yourself. Yet we share so many concerns as Black women, so much work to be done. The urgency of the destruction of our Black children and the theft of young Black minds are joint urgencies. Black children shot down or doped up on the streets of our cities are priorities for all of us. The fact of Black women's blood flowing with grim regularity in the streets and living rooms of Black communities is not a Black Lesbian rumor. It is sad statistical fact. The fact that there is a widening and dangerous lack of communication around our differences between Black women and men is not a Black Lesbian plot. It is a fact that becomes starkly clarified as we see our young people becoming more and more uncaring of each other. Young Black boys believing that they can define their manhood between a sixth grade girl's legs, growing up believing that Black women and girls are the fitting target for their justifiable furies rather than the racist structures grinding us all into dust, these are not Black Lesbian myths. These are sad realities of Black communities today and of immediate concern to us all. We cannot afford to waste each other's energies in our common battles.

What does homophobia mean? It means that high-powered Black women are told it is not safe to attend a Conference on the Status of Women in Nairobi simply because we are Lesbians. It means that in a political action, you rob yourselves of the vital insight and energies of political women such as Betty Powell and Barbara Smith and Gwendolyn Rogers and Raymina Mays and Robin Christian and Yvonne Flowers. It means another instance of the divide and conquer routine.

How do we organize around our differences, neither denying them nor blowing them up out of proportion?

The first step is an effort of will on your part. Try to remember to keep certain facts in mind. Black Lesbians are not apolitical. We have been a part of every freedom struggle within this country. Black Lesbians are not a threat to the Black family. Many of us have families of our own. We are not white, and we are not a disease. We are women who love women. This does not mean we are going to assault your daughters in an alley on Nostrand Avenue. It does not mean we are about to attack you if we pay you a compliment on your dress. It does not mean we only think about sex, any more than you only think about sex.

Even if you *do* believe any of these stereotypes about Black Lesbians, begin to practice *acting* like you don't believe them. Just as racist stereotypes are the problem of the white people who believe them, so also are homophobic stereotypes the problem of the heterosexuals who believe them. In other words, those stereotypes are yours to solve, not mine, and they are a terrible and wasteful barrier to our working together. I am not your enemy. We do not have to become each other's unique experiences and insights in order to share what we have learned through our particular battles for survival as Black Women . . .

There was a poster in the '60s that was very popular: HE'S NOT BLACK, HE'S MY BROTHER! It used to infuriate me because it implied that the two were mutually exclusive — "he" couldn't be both brother and Black. Well, I do not want to be tolerated, nor misnamed. I want to be recognized.

I am a Black Lesbian, and I *am* your sister.

I Am a Woman

Eyes on me daily
Frankly staring

My heel-less height
Wild natural hair, unadorned ears
and unfeminine clothes
Shock the eyes accustomed to the sight
of styled hair, make-up, and earrings.

I stand before the eyes wide with the question:
"Are you a man or a woman?"

The sex code broken.
The dress code defied.
And no slot to put me in.

It is an unwritten rule
that all female children must
have their ears pierced
That all women must
wear earrings.

If you don't believe this is a rule
Defy it as I do daily.

Jessie Fields, MD, is the Medical Director of the Chicago Center for Crisis Normalization and the Healthy Chicago Club. She is an attending physician at Cook County Hospital and an internist at the Harbor Light Freedom Center Medical Clinic. She went to medical school and did her residency at the Medical College of Pennsylvania. An accomplished poet, Jessie Fields is regularly published in journals and newspapers such as *Practice: The Journal of Politics, Economics, Psychology, Sociology & Culture*, *Blackout*, and *The Windy City Times*. Jessie has read her poetry at the Castillo Center in New York City, the Women's Coffee House in Chicago and the National Coalition of Black Lesbians and Gays Conference in 1985.

"I Am a Woman" first appeared in *Practice*, Vol. 4, No. 2, 1986. It is reprinted here with permission of the author and Practice Press, 7 East 20th Street, New York, NY 10003.

Stand with me
when someone calls me sir
Listen to me say
"I am a woman"
Watch them stare past me,
and continue to call me sir.
Listen to them say
"Women can't be that tall"
"You don't look like a woman"

How does a woman look?

I am a woman
A woman looks
like the woman she is.
I look like myself, a woman.
I define myself.
I define the woman I am.
And how this woman looks
And what this woman does
And who this woman loves
And I will be
no less than all of me.
I am a woman.

Jessie Fields

Asian-American Women: Psychological Responses to Sexual Exploitation and Cultural Stereotypes

Connie S. Chan

Much of the discussion concerning psychotherapy with Asian-Americans has focused upon the cultural differences, assimilation, and immigration history of Asian-American populations in the United States. Authors have pointed out that the Western therapeutic process is likely to be less effective for Asian-American clients because of different cultural norms concerning resistance and shame in the sharing of problems with mental health professionals (D. W. Sue, 1981; S. Sue, D. W. Sue, & D. Sue, 1975; Toupin, 1980).

The majority of the written material has discussed the many differences and conflicts between the American and Asian cultural norms which affect the therapeutic process for both male and female Asian-Americans clients. Little attention has been focused, however, upon the phenomenon of sexual exploitation and the gender-specific cultural stereotypes which are unique to the situation of Asian women in America. The existence of sexual exploitation in the form of mail order brides and the cultural stereotypes of Asian women as exotic sexual objects have an unknown, perhaps subtle effect upon Asian-American women in the United States. The psychological responses of Asian-American women to these factors are

Connie S. Chan, PhD, is Assistant Professor of Human Services at the College of Public and Community Services at the University of Massachusetts in Boston. She is also a clinical psychologist who specializes in bilingual/bicultural work in the Asian-American community.

varied, but it is important to examine these factors in the context of psychotherapy with Asian-American women.

What are some of the unique features of the sexual exploitation of Asian women, and how have the cultural stereotypes helped to develop this exploitation? To what extent are Asian-American women affected by these factors? What are the psychological responses adopted by Asian-American women, and what must a therapist be aware of while engaged in therapy with Asian-American women?

In addressing these issues, I will discuss the unique aspects of sexual exploitation of Asian women which have developed over time by examining the historical context and the cultural stereotypes which provide the breeding ground for racial and sexual discrimination. Then I will offer ways to help Asian-American women and psychotherapists develop an awareness of the psychological impact of these issues, and the ways of using them to empower themselves.

HISTORICAL CONTEXT

The colonization of many countries in Asia fostered a sense of ownership and a justification of superiority over another racial group, Asians, by the Western powers. Since the very imposition of colonization implies ownership, Asian people were perceived as commodities, as economic units of labor. Women, in a sexist world, occupied the lowest rung on the economic ladder and became the cheapest commodities.

Asian women were not only economic commodities, but sexual stereotypes developed to make women sexual commodities. During the U.S. involvement with the Philippines wars, Japan and China in World War II, and more recently, the Korean and Vietnamese Wars, Asian women were perceived by American soldiers as prostitutes and sexual objects who provided rest and recuperation from the war zones. This perception was not restricted to Western soldiers overseas, but was portrayed and perpetuated through film and other media in the United States and Europe. While Asian people were frequently shown as teeming, less than human masses in war movies, Asian women, shown in relation to a Western man, were almost always portrayed as exotic sexual objects. Sometimes the

Asian woman could be clever, conniving, or deceitful, but she tended to use her sexual prowess to achieve her goals, and was generally treated as a sexual object by the Western men.

As a result of these war and media images, Asian women have suffered from a cultural stereotype of being exotic, subservient, passive, sexually attractive and available. Films such as "Rambo" and the James Bond movies perpetuated these sexual stereotypes because there are such few visible Asian women represented in the print or audiovisual media in the U.S.

In addition, the phenomenon of the Asian mail order bride business demonstrates the objectification and fascination of white America with Asian women as submissive sexual servants. The very existence of this exploitative economic endeavor, and the lack of publicity or public outcry from Asian-American or women's organizations demonstrates a lack of awareness of the subtle negative psychological effects of this mail order business.

The mail order bride business has been in existence for over ten years. Mail order bride catalogs charge large sums of money to "match" available women from Asia (over one-half come from the Philippines and other Southeast Asian countries) with white Caucasian men who are mostly American, Canadian, and Australian. The Asian women tend to be young and poor women who seek to escape desperate economic poverty through marriage and immigration. When a contract is signed, the Asian mail order "bride" emigrates to the United States, where her immigration status is a tenuous one. She is a foreigner, not only to the new culture, language and society, but to her new husband's race and nationality as well. By any objective standards, the mail order bride business is an extremely unbalanced one in regard to power and access. There is no question that an Asian mail order bride is very vulnerable once she leaves her family and comes alone to an unknown husband; the potential for exploitation and abuse is great.

One Asian-American civil rights organization, the Japanese-American Citizens League, has been active in publicizing the mail order bride business as a racist, sexist enterprise. In their pamphlet, they note:

The reason businesses which exploit racial and sexual stereotypes such as the mail order bride catalogs exist, is due in part because of consistent media reinforcement of such stereotypes. The absence of significant positive models reinforces a damaging stereotype and invisibility of Asians in America. (JACL, 1985)

It is not only the Asian mail order brides who are victimized by sexual exploitation and cultural stereotypes, but *all* Asian women in America are affected by these perceptions. Asian-American women are, paradoxically, seen both as invisible, and as sexually attractive because of our race and gender. We are perceived as being quiet, submissive, willing to please, and even safe to pursue because we would not be likely to be rejecting. And because of cultural values that we as Asian-American women are brought up with and cherish, we *are* frequently agreeable, gentle, willing to please others before ourselves.

PSYCHOLOGICAL RESPONSES

In my clinical practice, I have worked with many Asian-American women who have struggled with the conflict of these cultural values: wanting to be true to their cultural upbringing, values that they believe in, and yet feeling abused, unrespected by the American cultural system which puts one's needs ahead of all others. While these women may be aware of the cultural differences which result in such conflicts, they are usually *unaware* of the gender and sexual stereotypes of Asian women which exacerbate these cultural conflicts. Instead, much of the subtle sexual harassment in the form of sexual innuendos, including propositions from bosses, feeling uncomfortable and objectified by men, etc., is repressed or initially denied.

When Asian-American women speak of their conflicts, they frequently focus first upon their familial relationships, then their work relationships, and only later upon their relationship with the rest of American society. It is when discussing their roles as Asian-American women that they become more aware of the way they are perceived by American cultural and sexual stereotypes. The initial psychological response is frequently a feeling of vulnerability and helplessness, a wish for both invisibility and yet seeking attention for whom they really are, a diverse group, not a stereotypical group. Most women are uncomfortable with the attention given to them as a result of their race and gender, so they seek little or no attention at all, in the hopes that this stereotyped attention will disappear. These are feelings of helplessness, of avoidance, of feeling guilty for being a victim. One Asian-American woman expressed this conflict in this way:

> I wanted to hide whenever a man told me I had beautiful almond-shaped eyes, or that I was such a petite little Asian doll. I never felt that I was being complimented for being myself, or the way *I* looked, but rather for being an Asian female who looked exotic. I stopped trusting any compliments, even ones which were not about my physical appearance. I felt more like an object, like someone else's idea of an Asian woman, than like a worthwhile person on my own. The worst part about it is that I felt it was my fault instead of the way others perceived me. I really felt I was unable to cope, and that I deserved to be unhappy.

This woman's story was not at all unusual. In a group of twelve Asian-American professional women, eleven expressed similar feelings of objectification and the accompanying feelings of distrust, worthlessness, and self-blame. Most remarkably, perhaps, each of these women blamed herself and felt that she was alone in her feelings of helplessness and vulnerability. None had perceived the problem to be external, based upon cultural and societal stereotypes, but all had internalized the problems as unique to herself. This group, which was not a therapy group, but was a discussion group of Asian-American women in their thirties, seemed to experience a great deal of relief and empowerment in their open discussion of these issues. These were topics which heretofore had been too personal, too vulnerable to discuss openly. There were many expressions of shame, of feelings of guilt, particularly around being a victim of sexual harassment and feeling objectified. While this is similar to the victim guilt syndrome experienced by survivors of sexual abuse, these Asian-American women had the extra burden of coping with racial and cultural stereotypes and oppression.

Awareness, education, openness, and confrontation of these stereotypes are effective in channeling the psychological responses from negative ones to positive ones. Asian-American women carry a double burden of racial and gender stereotyping. It has resulted in sexual exploitation on a global level, and mail order brides on an economic level. However, the heaviest toll may be on a personal level for Asian-American women who have internalized the cultural stereotypes which bind them. While psychological responses may seem limited to each woman on an individual basis, increased awareness of the external effects of sexual exploitation, inaccurate cultural stereotypes, and gender discrimination can provide other positive responses.

Asian-American women are finding their choices, their voices, and new responses, both on an individual basis, and collectively. As therapists, it is our responsibility to learn and to educate others about this sexual exploitation and cultural stereotyping; as women, both Asian-American and non-Asian, it is our task to actively work to reject the sexual/cultural stereotypes which oppress Asian-American women.

REFERENCES

JACL Women's Concerns Committee (1980). Mail order Asian women catalogues: Report issued by the Japanese-American citizens league, Spring 1985.

Krich, J. (1986). Here come the brides. *Mother Jones*, Feb/March 1986, 34-37, 43-46.

Serita, T. (1984). Mail order sexploitation, *BRIDGE, 9*(2), 25-28.

Sue, D.W. (1981). Cultural and historical perspectives in counseling Asian Americans. In D. Sue (Ed.), *Counseling the culturally different* (pp. 113-140), New York: John Wiley & Sons.

Sue, S., Sue, D.W., Sue, D. (1975). Asian Americans as a minority group. *American Psychologist, 31*, 906-910.

Toupin, E. (1980). Counseling Asians: Psychotherapy in the context of racism and Asian-American history. *American Journal of Orthopsychiatry, 50*(1), 76-86.

Villapando, V. (1986). Asian mail order brides: A growing phenomenon. *The Hawaii Herald*, Feb. 7, 1986, 6-11.

Feminist Therapy
with Hispanic/Latina Women:
Myth or Reality?

Lillian Comas-Díaz

INTRODUCTION

The relevance of feminist therapy to ethnic minority populations has been questioned. Most of these concerns arise from criticisms of the earlier feminist philosophy. Ethnic minority women's alienation from the feminist movement stems from the women's movement's emphasis on the paid labor force and the subsequent escape from the confines of the home (Dill, 1983). Such emphasis is foreign to many women of color, who have worked all of their lives and will continue to do so. In their discussion of feminist therapy's relevance to Black and Hispanic populations, Mays and Comas-Díaz (in press) state that ethnic minority women's criticism of feminism arises out of two beliefs: (1) women's oppression is the most fundamental oppression, and (2) sisterhood asserts that a female has more in common with another female regardless of ethnic, racial, or socioeconomic group. These feminist beliefs tend to neglect the crucial role that ethnicity, culture, race, and socioeconomic class play in the lives of women of color. This article examines the application of feminist therapy to Hispanic/Latina women.

Lillian Comas-Díaz is the former Director of the Yale Department of Psychiatry Hispanic Clinic and the former Director of the American Psychological Association's office of Ethnic Minority Affairs. Currently, Dr. Comas-Díaz is the Co-Director of the Trans-Cultural Mental Health Institute in Washington, DC, where she also has a private practice. She has published extensively on psychotherapy with emphasis on ethnic minority women and transcultural psychotherapy. Dr. Comas-Díaz is involved with Amnesty International and went to Chile to investigate the effects of abuses of human rights on mental health.

39

FEMINIST THERAPY
AND HISPANIC/LATINA WOMEN

Ethnicity and feminism have been opposing forces. Due to survival issues, many ethnic minority women tend to be more committed to their ethnic identity as opposed to their political identity as
women (Dill, 1983). Moreover, their overriding commitment is
with the improvement of their ethnic/racial group, for both female
and male members. Takooshian and Stuart (1983) further discuss
the conflict prevalent between feminism and ethnicity. They argue
that ethnic women tend to resist feminism because it is egalitarian,
universalistic, and moves from an imperfect present to a more per-
fect future. Conversely, ethnicity emphasizes group differences, it
is particularistic, and seems to rely more on a traditional past.

The question remains: Is feminist therapy relevant to Hispanic/
Latina women? or, Is the application of feminist therapy to His-
panic/Latina women a myth or a reality? There has been an increased awareness in feminism among Latin American women.
These women are questioning their roles vis-à-vis the oppression
that they experience imposed by their male counterparts (Costello,
1977). Moreover, Latin American writers are viewing feminism as
a process leading towards women's emancipation from their second
class citizenship (Zayas & Silén, 1972). Defined as a set of political, economic and social values which support balanced power relations between the sexes, feminism is potentially relevant to all
women. However, in order to be effective with Hispanic women,
this perspective needs to be culturally embedded.

Current feminist therapy is conceptualized as a pluralistic, integrative, and dialectical perspective that has the potential to accommodate the complex, unique, and changing needs of Hispanic
women. It calls for a dialectical relationship between its theory and
practice. Current feminist therapy is not restricted by any particular
theoretical orientation. It is a perspective that integrates feminist
philosophy into theory, practice and ethical standards of traditional
psychotherapies (Douglas & Walker, in press). As an interactive
process, feminist therapy allows for the accommodation of the
ethno-sociocultural variables, political influences, and women's intrapsychic realities, and their consequent impact on the etiology,

presentation, expectations, and approach to treatment of women of color (Mays & Comas-Díaz, in press).

Feminist therapy also entails a commitment to social change. When working with Hispanic/Latina women, as well as with other women of color, social change acquires pivotal relevance. Delivering services to Hispanic women requires an understanding of the sociopolitical forces that shape their lives, and demands an active involvement of these issues in treatment. Such a perspective examines the unique experiences of Hispanic women, acknowledging the influence that society has on them.

In the author's clinical experience, using feminist therapy with Hispanic women can potentially result in a greater awareness and understanding of the oppressive effects of traditional sex role while functioning within the mainstream society. This approach also helps Latinas with their adaptation to cultural change, and offers them a more functional coping style. Hispanic/Latina women become more aware of their oppressive situations, explore more options, and are empowered to make informed decisions.

Feminist therapy can be perceived as a means of empowerment for Hispanic women. Given their long history of oppression, this perspective could help Hispanic women in their liberation process. The process of empowerment within the feminist psychotherapeutic context is identified by Mays and Comas-Díaz (in press) as helping women of color to:

1. acknowledge the deleterious effects of sexism and racism;
2. deal with feelings of anger and self degradation imposed by their status of ethnic minorities;
3. perceive themselves as causal agents in achieving solutions to their problems;
4. understand the interplay between the external environment and their inner reality; and
5. perceive opportunities to change the responses from the wider society.

A sixth factor that needs to be added to the empowerment of Hispanic women within the feminist psychotherapeutic context is the acknowledgment of the deleterious effects of elitism. Among the diverse Hispanic/Latino populations in the United States, social class becomes a differential variable. Latin American countries, like many other Third World countries, have clear demarcations along social class lines. In fact, many Latin American countries do not have a middle class as we know it in the United States. Thus, elitist attitudes, based on the dichotomous social class divisions, are transplanted to the United States. Feminist therapy, with its emphasis on social context, can help Hispanic/Latina women to identify their own elitism and prejudices, to confront the elitism that they may be subjected to by their own cultural group, and to develop a more egalitarian perspective.

Empowerment for Hispanic/Latina women also involves the satisfactory negotiation of conflictive cultural demands. For many Latinas this entails coping with culture change, acculturation, and biculturalism. More specifically, the process of empowerment helps to achieve the successful negotiation of traditional sex roles, with the changing sexual mores, and with the emergence of new ones. Notwithstanding these issues, feminist therapy requires the integration of a sociocultural perspective in order to be effective with the Hispanic female. Let us examine some of these variables.

SOCIALIZATION AND DEVELOPMENTAL ISSUES

The wide diversity among the Hispanic/Latino populations in the United States constitutes a mosaic. Hispanics are multicultural, multiracial, and multiethnic. Some of them have recently immigrated, while others have been in the U.S. since long before the arrival of the Pilgrims. Hispanics is a generic term used by the U.S. Bureau of the Census to designate persons of Spanish origin or descent, or those who designate themselves as Mexican, Mexican American, Chicano, Puerto Rican, Boricua, Cuban, or other Spanish/Hispanic. Some Hispanics designate themselves as Latinos, stressing their Latin American background. Regardless of self-designation, their attachment to the Hispanic culture and Spanish language is strong. While they share a common bond of cultural background, language, and religion, the different Hispanic groups have distinct profiles. Each group has its own perceptions of itself, other Hispanic/Latin groups, and of its place in the United States.

Hispanic/Latina women share a stronger and deeper common bond. Espín (1986) has identified this bond as resulting from four elements: *Historical influences* (colonization by Spain, cultural background), the experience of *separation by (im)migration*, the cognitive and affective effects of sharing a *common language*, and the experience of *oppression*. Obviously, this bond is further strengthened by the experience of being female within the Hispanic/Latino context.

Gender Issues

One feminist premise is that the socialization of women differs from that of men and that this socialization is destructive and oppressive to women. Let us examine its relevance to the Hispanic/Latino culture. Traditionally, the Hispanic family is patriarchal, with an authoritarian father, a "submissive" mother, and a mutual acceptance of this pattern. Throughout Latin America, San Martin (1975) found women's subordination to men's authority well-accepted.

Boys and girls are taught early on two very different codes of sexual behavior. Traditional Hispanic women are expected to be sentimental, gentle, intuitive, impulsive, docile, submissive, dependent and timid; while men are expected to be cold, intellectual, rational, profound, strong, authoritarian, independent, and brave (Senour, 1977). This rigid demarcation of sex roles encourages a double moral standard for the sexes, exemplified in the *marianismo/machismo* syndrome.

The concept underlying *marianismo* is based on the Catholic worship of the Virgin Mary, who is both a virgin and a madonna. *Marianismo* predicates that women are spiritually superior to men, and therefore capable of enduring all suffering inflicted by men (Stevens, 1973).

Taught to follow the Virgin Mary as their ultimate model, unmarried women are expected to be chaste and virginal and not to demonstrate interest in sex once they are married. When they become mothers, Hispanic women attain the status of madonnas and, accordingly, are expected to sacrifice in favor of their children and husbands. The self-sacrifice maxim is very common in the Hispanic/Latina culture. For example, the image of the *Mater Dolorosa* is prevalent among Mexican American women, who without being masochistic, appear to obtain satisfaction and fulfillment from "suffering" (Bach y Rita, 1982).

The counterpart of *marianismo* is *machismo*. This sex role literally means maleness or virility, but culturally it means that the man is the provider and responsible for the welfare, honor, and protection of the family. In its extreme form, *machismo* is manifested through physical dominance of women and excessive alcohol consumption (Giraldo, 1972). Furthermore, *machismo* dictates that the Hispanic male must constantly signal his sexual availability; seductive behavior is mandatory regardless of marital status (Sluzki, 1982). Paradoxically, the *macho* must protect his female relatives from the sexual advances of other men while making as many sexual conquests as possible. Though it has been argued that *machismo* is more prevalent among lower socioeconomic classes (Kinzer, 1973), it is nevertheless believed to influence behavior in all strata of the Hispanic/Latin American society (Giraldo, 1972).

Machismo has also been examined from a psychodynamic perspective. Aramoni (1982) argues that *machismo* can be perceived as men's effort to compensate for their overpresent, powerfully demanding and suffering mothers, as well as an identification with their psychologically absent fathers. More recently, *machismo* has been examined from a socioeconomic and historical perspective, emphasizing more its characteristics as provider and supporter (both financially and emotionally) of the family members (De La Cancela, 1986).

A third sex role prevalent among some Hispanic/Latina women is *hembrismo*, which literally means femaleness. *Hembrismo* has been described as a cultural revenge to machismo (Habach, 1972). According to Gomez (1982), a male psychiatrist, *hembrismo* is a frustrated attempt to imitate a male, resulting in a primitive or rough female. This imitation occurs in a sociosexual spectrum of idealized roles, becoming a natural reaction within a historical context. Gomez further posits that *hembrismo* shares common elements with the women's movement in the areas of social and political goals.

Comas-Díaz (1982) discusses *hembrismo* within the Puerto Rican society. She argues that *hembrismo* acknowledges the powerful position that the female has in her culture. The indigenous Puerto Ricans, the Taíno Indians, had a matriarchal society, under which family name, property, and tribal leadership were inherited through the females (Steiner, 1974). However, females did not utilize their power to oppress males. The females' strong influence was further strengthened by spiritual power. Females had the power to invoke the spirits, which attributed an extraordinary importance to the female in an island ruled by the "earth mother concept" (Fernández-Méndez, 1972).

Presently, *hembrismo* connotes strength, perseverance, flexibility, and an ability for survival. However, it can be translated into the woman's attempt to fulfill her multiple roles expectations as a mother, wife, worker, daughter, member of the community, etc.; in other words, the *superwoman* working the *double jornada* (double day; working at home and outside the home). This situation can precipitate stress and emotional problems for the woman behaving in the *hembrista* fashion. On the other hand, *hembrismo* can also explain the strength, motivation, and will power that characterize Hispanic females.

Acculturation

The construct of acculturation acquires a crucial significance while working with Hispanic/Latina women. Studies of immigrant families indicate that ethnic values and identification with the culture of origin are retained for many generations after the immigration has occurred (Greeley, 1981) and so, too, the impact of the translocation are manifest in clinical situations several generations after the move (Sluzki, 1979). For instance, sex roles among Hispanic women in the United States can be complicated (and confused) by the expectations imposed by the two different cultural contexts in which they operate. The Anglo culture tends to apply "masculine" criteria to the evaluation of women, ascribing the greatest value to those who distinguish themselves occupationally or professionally. Yet this tendency is contradicted enough to send mixed messages to the female. Consequently, for example, the Chicana is far surer of her role within the traditional Mexican American culture than she is in the mainstream, where her role is ambivalent

(Senour, 1977). Apparently, this sureness of role that her Hispanic culture provides has not stopped the Chicana, nor other Latina women in the midst of cultural change, from exploring the behavioral alternatives available to her. This experimentation can lead to conflict within the nuclear unit as well as within the extended family. Feminist therapy can help Hispanic women to deal with these contradictions and help them distinguish the societal pressures from their ethnocultural realities, from their personal dynamics.

The diverse degrees of acculturation need to be examined in treatment, as they are often related to gender roles. To illustrate, Torres-Matrullo (1980) found a significant relationship between level of acculturation, level of education and family and sex role attitudes among mainland Puerto Rican women. Findings indicated that the traditional concepts of womanhood appeared to be changing toward a more egalitarian model due to the increased education and exposure to the American society, but that the sacredness of motherhood remained as a cultural value.

Several reactions to culture change and acculturation among Hispanic/Latina women have been reported. Within a psychotherapeutic context, Comas-Díaz (1982) discussed three reactions to acculturation which are described as fluid coping styles. Low in the acculturation spectrum is the culturally marginal woman who has limited contact with the mainstream society. Typical of this category is the Hispanic woman who (im)migrated during her middle age, has limited education, is Spanish monolingual, and rigidly adheres to her cultural values, resistant to change. The second classification is characterized by high acculturation and assimilation, to the point of denying the Hispanic ethnic identity. Women in this position may self-identify as "American," "Black," "Italian," "Spaniard" or other. The third reaction, labeled the *cultural schizophrenic* model, consists of the woman who has some degree of acculturation who operates within the two cultures. At times she acts as a cultural bridge, and at others, she is confused by conflicting values. Under stress this woman could exhibit *cultural schizophrenia* as opposed to her regular functioning, when she successfully integrates aspects of both cultures. The *culturally schizophrenic* woman could eventually synthesize both cultures, achieving a new integrative cultural repertoire.

These typologies are not exhaustive. For instance, some Hispanic/Latina women are what is known as *culturally amphibious*, or being equally able to live in the Hispanic as well as in the American culture. These women usually can "pass" (are light skinned, do not have an accent, etc.), are bilingual and bicultural and, like amphibious animals, can live in two different environments without difficulties. Some of these women remain in their amphibious state, and others move to a different classification, depending on their developmental stage or political status. Some of them could vicariously experience racism, ethnocentrism, and/or directly confront sexism. These experiences may raise their political consciousness, leading to self-identification as Hispanic/Latina women. *Culturally amphibious* women differ from *culturally schizophrenic* women in that they can choose which environment to live in, without having others impose ethnic definitions on them.

Hispanic/Latina females continue to face acculturation conflicts within an intergenerational framework. For example, a first generation woman, a second generation one, and a recently (im)migrated woman are placed in different positions within the acculturation spectrum. However, as suggested in Torres-Matrullo's (1980) research, these women could be experiencing gender roles conflicts. Within this framework, gender roles need to be assessed and the socioeconomic context considered. For example, a middle class first generation *marianista* woman may profess progressive and even feminist views on women's education and employment, while holding traditional values on marital relationships. These types of paradoxes comprise the fabric of Hispanic/Latina women's position in their culture.

POWER AND OPPRESSION

At first blush the traditional Hispanic sexual roles seem to condone the oppression of one group (female) by another (male), thus being consistent with the feminist precept that the socialization process is destructive and oppressive to women. However, the dynamics involved in the male-female relations are complicated and deceiving. The sexual power relationship is not apparent. For instance, Stevens (1973) asserts that the *marianista* code rewards women who adhere to it. Because motherhood is sacred, women who bear children enjoy a certain degree of power despite the outward submissiveness of their behavior. Conversely, women who do not conform to the code risk social censorship. As a consequence, a dichotomous classification of women is reinforced, i.e., the Madonna/whore complex.

In the United States, Hispanic women are observed to defend and thus perpetuate *machismo* as a way of protecting the egos of their male relatives from the socioeconomic and political humiliations they suffer. For instance, Senour (1977) claims Chicanas reinforce *machismo* in their men to compensate for their lack of status in the Anglo culture. Similarly, Steiner (1974) cites Puerto Rican women who defend *machismo* as an understandable response to deprivation in the economic, social and political spheres; men take their frustrations out on women because they cannot have power elsewhere. This may be an example of Hispanic women's support of their ethnic identities as opposed to their (gender) political ones. While utilizing a feminist perspective, the therapist needs to be aware of these dynamics.

Traditional sex roles are undergoing change among Hispanics in the United States. For one thing, the Hispanic culture, including its *machismo/marianismo* precepts, is not reinforced by the new dominant culture, which, in fact, is pervaded by the impact of the women's movement. Furthermore, the act of (im)migration (whether recent or generations ago) itself often presents Hispanic men and women with a sexual role reversal which impacts the whole family system. In studies of recent immigrant families it has been observed that the family member who most often deals with the dominant culture assumes the instrumental role, thus becoming increasingly isolated (Sluzki, 1979). Not surprisingly, in many cases the instrumental role is filled by the male; the affective one by the female. Though this split between partners in cultural transition can result in imbalanced power, and in mental health and marital problems (Canino, 1982a), the division of labor, so to speak, is in keeping with the traditional sex role expectations in Hispanic culture.

Instrumental/affective role-taking is not always respectively male/female, however. The pressures of economic survival in the new culture, as well as the type of skills that are marketable, have caused a role reversal among Hispanics. In fact, this role reversal is by no means rare, as it is often easier for female immigrants to obtain employment in the United States than it is for males. Indeed, the woman may have no choice but to assume the instrumental role because she is able to sell her sewing and domestic skills while her husband's ability to farm does him no good in the city. Consequently, the Hispanic woman's access to and ability to come to terms with mainstream American society can be much quicker and easier than for the man. Financial independence offers control and power to the Hispanic female. Feminist therapy, with its emphasis on power-balanced relationships, can be used effectively to address some of these issues.

Another illustration of the deceiving appearance of the power relations between Latino males and females is presented by a study of gender roles among Hispanics in the United States. Canino (1982b) found that on the surface, both husband and wife reported espousing traditional attitudes. However, when the same couples were interviewed more extensively, and observations were made during the decision making process, the most prevalent marital transaction found was a shared process. Although most of the couples studied by Canino were Puerto Ricans, her findings are relevant to other Hispanic populations as well. Likewise, among Mexican American couples, the decision-making process is also deceiving. Falicov (1982) reports that Mexican American families may include husbands who are domineering and patriarchal, those who are submissive and dependent upon their wives for making major decisions, as well as families who have an egalitarian power structure. These research findings and clinical observations suggest that the cultural context needs to be considered when asserting that the socialization process is oppressive to Hispanic/Latina women.

Another female way of obtaining power is for Latinas to emphasize their culturally ascribed feminine role. Historically, women in most cultures have used healing and magic as a means of empowerment (Bourguignon, 1979). Likewise, the Hispanic culture assigns the healing role to women. Females are overrepresented in the folk healing process: *curanderas* among Mexican American women, *espiritistas* among Puerto Ricans, and *santeras* among Cubans. Espin (1984) conducted a study of Hispanic female healers in the United States. She found that these women obtain power by virtue of their healing abilities. They are transformed from powerless members in the family, due to the traditional sex roles expectations, to the most powerful ones. These women perform behaviors that are usually associated with feminism. For instance, they exert control over their lives by leaving their families in order to pursue their healing careers, and as a consequence, achieve social mobility, financial independence, and community prestige.

Hispanic/Latina women enjoy a combination of powerlessness and power. This paradox is exemplified by the sexual roles of *marianismo* and *hembrismo*. For example, Hispanic cultural dynamics discourage females' direct expression of their feelings (especially negative) and rights. As an illustration, the concept of assertiveness does not have a literal translation in Spanish. Furthermore, the culture reinforces women's roles as secondary to men's. Espin (1986) asserts that although Hispanic women consider men to be undependable and untrustworthy, many of them remain in an abusive relationship because having a man is an important source of the female's self-esteem. Similarly, feelings of inferiority, premature marriages and motherhood among Hispanic women have been related to the traditional female roles (Canino, 1982a).

Feminist therapy could be useful in assessing and working through this paradox. As daughters of oppression, Hispanic/Latina females may utilize indirect and/or covert manipulation techniques in order to exert power in a culturally acceptable manner. For instance, Stevens (1973) asserts that when *marianista* women grow older, they attain a semi-divine status. Within this context, adult offspring fight their mothers' struggles, especially against their fathers. The women manipulate their children into doing what they want, and thus, exert control over their husbands. In this case, power is achieved through passivity, conformity to the *marianista* code, and indirect/covert manipulation. López-Garrida (1978) describes the use of indirect and/or covert manipulation among Puerto Rican women, asserting that these strategies are characteristic of all oppressed people regardless of gender and/or ethnicity. Feminist therapy, with its commitment to social change, could help Hispanic/Latina women negotiate a more functional way of expressing their needs.

CLINICAL APPLICATIONS

While utilizing feminist therapy with Hispanic/Latina women, the therapist needs to understand this group's help-seeking behaviors and treatment expectations. The Hispanic/Latino culture does not differentiate between physical and emotional concerns (Padilla & Ruiz, 1973). As an example of this interrelationship, strong emotions are believed to cause physical illness (Maduro, 1983). Therefore the mental state affects the physical condition and vice versa. This cultural tendency is consistent with Hispanic women's style of indirect communication. Many Hispanic/Latina women tend to report somatic complaints as a means of expressing their needs, and thereby obtaining support from significant others (Hynes & Werbin, 1977). Likewise, in noting the high incidence of somatic complaints among low-income Hispanic women in psychotherapy, Espín (1985) suggests that these complaints may well be a reaction to the self-sacrifice dictum, especially since somatization is a culturally accepted mode of expressing needs and feelings.

The body/mind interrelation has helped to reinforce the stereotype that Hispanics are not psychologically minded. However, an investigation conducted by Comas-Díaz and her associates (1982) reported that Hispanics requesting services at a community mental health clinic presented complaints of a psychological nature, including depression, anxiety, concentration problems, obsessions and compulsions, fears, and sleep problems. They also complained of physical and financial problems, consistent with their holistic approach to health and illness. These specific requests responded to the socioeconomic and cultural contexts in which many of these clients live. The results were analyzed by gender, yielding a higher report of drug problems, antisocial behavior, and suicidality among Hispanic males. The researchers concluded that the overall findings challenge previous perceptions of Hispanics which have portrayed such clients as unsuitable for intensive psychotherapy due to their emphasis on defining their mental health problems as somatic or medical rather than psychological in nature.

The investigation also studied Hispanic clients' expectations regarding treatment and their therapist. Findings indicated that Hispanics expected the therapist to be decisive and give advice, while viewing themselves as active participants and assuming personal responsibility for the outcome of therapy. Hispanic clients showed grounding in psychological precepts in that they accept unconscious feelings and ambivalence towards others. These clients also acknowledged the importance and the value of expressing thoughts and feelings. They expressed a desire for a therapeutic relationship in which they may talk freely about themselves and their problems; this extended, as well, to their thoughts and feelings. Moreover, they reported a willingness to persist in this type of experience despite the fact that it is apt to be distressing at times. In sum, Hispanic clients expressed a complex set of treatment expectations including psychological, medical, and environmental variables.

A feminist perspective is highly appropriate for these clients, given that this philosophy regards the individual's behavior as best understood by examining the social structure. Within this context, feminist therapy is able to address Hispanic women's complex nature of expectations and attitudes toward psychotherapy.

CASE VIGNETTES

The following cases illustrate the application of feminist therapy with Hispanic/Latina women. These vignettes present Latina women from different Hispanic ethnic groups, indicating varying degrees of success with this perspective. Clients' identifying data have been altered to protect confidentiality. In all case vignettes the therapist was the author, a Hispanic/Latina (Puerto Rican) clinical psychologist.

Elba, a 35-year-old Cuban woman, is divorced and has a ten-year-old daughter. She was born in Cuba, and moved to the United States when she was five years old. Elba is bilingual, well educated

(Master's degree), and occupies the position of director of public relations in a major business institution.

Elba came to therapy due to her internist's referral for her "panic attacks." Her previous lover had tested positive for the AIDS virus, but did not have the disease. Although she tested negative, Elba was experiencing severe panic attacks. Furthermore, she was very hurt because she had been monogamous while her lover had been seeing other people. She also terminated that relationship and was mourning its loss.

Clinical evaluation revealed that the client's panic attacks occurred around the period of her going to see the physician. Elba had created a vicious circle, where she wanted to be tested for the AIDS virus every two months, and then would develop panic attacks waiting for the tests' results. Collaboration with her internist helped to gain control over the frequency of her testing (she did not need to be tested that frequently).

The first stage of therapy concentrated on alleviating Elba's presenting complaints. She responded well to behavior techniques, and her panic attacks subsided. During this time, Elba revealed that she started to date another man, and that she had not told him about her ex-lover's AIDS tests' positive findings. She stated that given her negative tests' results, her physician did not advise her to tell her boyfriend. Therapy then helped Elba to decide the course of the relationship (whether to tell him about her own exposure to the AIDS virus, or to terminate the relationship). The feminist premise of power-balanced relationship between the sexes helped Elba to cope with this immediate situation. She expressed fears of loosing her current boyfriend, but simultaneously, was feeling upset about not being honest with him. Elba, who was *culturally amphibious*, was fearing that her boyfriend, an Anglo male, would be prejudicial and blame the AIDS situation on her ethnicity. Hence, feminist orientation explored her feelings of self-degradation resulting from her belonging to an ethnic minority group.

The feminist therapeutic perspective also helped Elba to examine the alternatives available to her and their consequences. The client decided to communicate to her boyfriend about her exposure to the

AIDS virus. His reaction was to be initially shocked, and after-
wards, to have the AIDS testing. After finding that his results were
negative he decided to continue his relationship with Elba.

After this crisis was managed, Elba began feeling guilty for having had sex with a bisexual man. Indeed, she reported feeling guilty
for all of her previous sexual behavior. Elba's strict Catholic background was influencing her reaction to this crisis. She believed that
she would be punished (by contracting AIDS) for her sexual behavior (which she identified as licentious). In addition, she was preoc-
cupied with the idea that when "people find out, they will think that
I am a whore." Elba was referring to the Cuban community. (According to Bernal [1982] within the Cuban contemporary cultural
context, women are often dichotomized into being pure like the
Virgin Mary, and those who are not "pure," are labelled whores.)
Thus, the cultural setting offered a reality-based context to the client's preoccupations with being a whore.

A feminist perspective helped Elba to examine the oppressive
effects of the traditional Hispanic/Cuban sex roles socialization.
This approach, coupled with a cognitive-behavioral orientation,
was used to help Elba deal with her distorted cognitions regarding
her sexual behavior. After eight months in therapy, Elba was no
longer experiencing panic attacks, had reassessed her relationship
with her boyfriend, and began to examine her ethnic self-identification. Moreover, partly due to feminism's guiding principle of social
action, Elba was working with a group aimed at increasing the
awareness of AIDS within the Hispanic/Latin community.

The following vignette presents a case of a Mexican American
second generation woman who is struggling with non-traditional
sex roles.

Lourdes is a 29-year-old single, second generation Mexican
American law student. She is the eldest offspring from a low income family of five, and the first one to go into graduate school.
Lourdes presented to treatment complaining of mild depression,
difficulties in concentrating, and falling behind her work in school.
Lourdes was enrolled in an Ivy League university, and felt severe
pressure to perform well, in order to "set the example" for her
siblings. The client initially presented to treatment with a clinical
picture consistent with a role transition problem. Lourdes was hav-

ing difficulties adjusting to her new role of graduate student after being out of college and working for several years.

After a psychiatric consultation yielded no biological basis for her depressive reaction, Lourdes was treated with interpersonal psychotherapy for depression (Klerman et al., 1984). The initial phase of therapy helped Lourdes to better cope with her adjustment to her new role. She stated that she was involved with the university's Chicano Studies Program and that she was politically active in the Chicano movement. This network seemed to be the only support system available to her. However, Lourdes continued complaining of feeling lonely.

After the therapeutic relationship was cemented, Lourdes began to express concerns regarding her adult developmental stage. She stated that she wanted to get married and have children, and felt pressured by her "biological clock." Given the emergence of this new issue, the therapist decided to perform an interpersonal inventory. While using this systematic and detailed exploration of the client's important relationships with significant others, Lourdes revealed that she was actually struggling with her sexual preference. She stated that she was a lesbian but that she had inhibited her sexual behavior because she was concerned about the effects of her behavior on her "poor suffering mother" (client's own words).

The client was a *culturally schizophrenic* woman who had been trying to integrate conflictive elements of the Mexican American and Anglo cultures. Within the confines of her family, Lourdes behaved very "Mexican American," being concerned about the implications of her lesbianism on her family. Additionally, she was fearful of the reaction that the cultural/political Chicano network would have if she "came out of the closet." This situation created a conflict with her expression of sexuality and her identity as a politically active Chicana.

Lourdes' concerns about her family and her cultural group's reactions to her lesbianism were well founded. The Hispanic/Latin culture tends to reject lesbianism. A study conducted by Hidalgo and Christensen (1976), examined the interactions and conflicts between Puerto Rican lesbians and the mainland Puerto Rican community. It is believed that this investigation's findings can be generalized to other Hispanic groups as well. The researchers found that

the Puerto Rican culture rejects lesbianism and makes it very difficult for the women to "come out." The majority of the professional
women who were lesbians indicated that they were not willing to
take the risk of "being found out" for fear that their leadership
position within the Puerto Rican community would be jeopardized.
Regarding the families of lesbians, the study found that although
they suspected the women's sexual preference, they pretended not
to know, and that many succumbed to societal pressures (such as,
"What will so-and-so think?").

Lourdes utilized therapy to cope with her depressive symptoms
resulting from her role transitions. She also decided to explore her
sexual preference and to examine her options as well as their consequences. Feminist therapy, with its emphasis on achieving meaning
in the individual's life, helped her to arrive at an informed decision.
Lourdes decided to express her sexuality via her lesbianism, but
through living a double life. She stated that she would not "adver-
tise" that she was lesbian, but that she would not deny it either.
However, she decided to actively hide this aspect of her life from
her family, and expressed no longer feeling guilty about her family's potential reaction if they ever found out. The combined use of
short-term interpersonal psychotherapy for depression and a feminist perspective helped Lourdes to examine her sexuality within a
cultural context, and to make a decision relevant for her.

The following vignette illustrates the case of a first generation
middle-aged Puerto Rican woman facing a conflict of sex role values.

Carmen is a 44-year-old first generation divorced Puerto Rican
woman. She has two adult children, ages 19 (female) and 21
(male). She is bilingual and works in a department store. Carmen
entered therapy upon a friend's recommendation. She was having
interpersonal problems with her co-workers. During the clinical
evaluation, Carmen complained of problems at work, stating that
the other women were "jealous" of her because she was promoted
to a supervisory position. Carmen had been promoted before, but
this was the first time that she experienced these types of problems.
Her interpersonal difficulties were characterized by Carmen's involvement in verbal arguments with female co-workers. Due to this

behavior she had received a reprimand at work, and thus she was afraid of lōsing her position.

Carmen was from a working class background, and although she only had a high school education, she was significantly successful in her work. She expressed pride in her work accomplishments and stated that she "did it all for her children." Indeed, based on Carmen's description of her life, it sounded as if she was behaving in a *marianista* fashion, by being self-sacrificing in favor of her children.

The therapist reviewed Carmen's significant relationships. It was revealed that she was involved with a Puerto Rican married man whom she felt very close to. Carmen described him as a very liberated man: "He is an *independentista*" (a believer in independence for Puerto Rico; a leftist). Carmen identified herself as a liberated woman who did not want to get married again, thus expressing satisfaction with her current sexual arrangement.

Therapy helped Carmen to examine her communication style with others. At work, Carmen had been vocal regarding women's rights and this behavior had made her a popular advocate for women in her work place. Within this context, her communication style was consistent and assertive. However, in her personal life, Carmen used mixed messages, plus covert and indirect communication patterns. A feminist perspective was utilized, helping Carmen to sort out the effects of her cultural context, societal variables (sexism and racism) and her own intrapersonal issues on her identified problem area. During this stage in treatment, Carmen began to express dissatisfaction with her sexual relationship. She was feeling used by her lover because she was in the position of *la querida* (mistress). Carmen expressed sadness and anger at this realization.

Initially, Carmen was pleased with her *independentista* lover and attributed to him progressive qualities in his sex role attitudes. However, she was ambivalent as to her own expectations from the relationship. Although she self-identified as a liberated woman, Carmen functioned under a *marianista* model. Within this context, the *querida* is considered a whore in the Puerto Rican society. She expressed shame and concern for the "bad example" that she was modeling to her daughter. Carmen's true expectations were to get married to her lover, but she did not communicate these to him. In fact, she got caught between her own traditional sex roles beliefs in her personal life, and her liberated, *hembrista* style in her public life.

Therapy incorporated a feminist perspective with a psychody-namic approach. Carmen was able to understand that some of her interpersonal problems with her female co-workers (who all hap-pened to be married) were partly a reflection of her anger within her sexual arrangement. Therapy helped Carmen to work through these feelings. The feminist perspective, with its aim at achieving mean-ing in the individual's life, helped Carmen to decide what she really wanted out of a love relationship. Through the aid of a decision analysis within the feminist perspective, the client decided that she wanted a formal commitment and not the role of *la querida*. When her lover refused to obtain a divorce, Carmen decided to terminate the relationship.

DISCUSSION

These three clinical vignettes present Hispanic women from dif-ferent Latin American origins: Cuban, Mexican American, and Puerto Rican. They also represent different socioeconomic classes: Elba was from a high middle class, Lourdes from a low socioeco-nomic status, but attending graduate school, and Carmen was from a working class background. These women also had different de-grees of acculturation. Elba was a *culturally amphibious* woman, and both Lourdes and Carmen were *culturally schizophrenic*; how-ever, Carmen was more on the Hispanic range of acculturation than Lourdes. Notwithstanding this diversity, there is a common bond that unites these women. All of them were struggling with cultural conflicts concerning their sex roles. Regardless of acculturation and socioeconomic class membership, these women carried remnants of their cultural baggage. Additionally, they were family and commu-nity oriented. Feminist orientation with its guiding principle of the importance of collective, was able to address their special needs. This perspective was successfully used in combination with behav-ioral-cognitive and interpersonal approaches, and psychodynamic orientations.

CONCLUSION

This article has examined the question of whether the application of feminist therapy to Hispanic/Latina women is a myth or a reality. It concludes by asserting that feminist therapy is effective when it is culturally embedded. With its precept of power-balanced relations between the sexes, its emphasis on the collective, and the importance of the social context, feminist therapy is highly relevant for Hispanic/Latina women. This perspective can potentially address the complex, unique and multiple needs of this population. Furthermore, as a dialectical process, feminist therapy can enable Hispanic/Latina women to examine culture change, the process of acculturation, and their impact on identity. Finally, this perspective can help Hispanic/Latina females in their liberation process. As daughters of oppression they can become empowered to examine various options, expand their alternatives, and make informed and more meaningful decisions affecting their lives and those of their significant others.

REFERENCES

Aramoni, A. (1982). Machismo. *Psychology Today, 5*(8), 69-72.

Bach y Rita, G. (1982). The Mexican American: Religion and cultural influences. In R. M. Becerra, M. Karno, & J. Escobar (Eds.) *Mental health and Hispanic Americans* (pp. 29-40). New York: Grune and Stratton.

Bernal, G. (1982). Cuban families. In M. McGoldrick, J.K. Pearce, & J. Giordano (Eds.) *Ethnicity and family therapy* (pp. 187-207). New York: The Guilford Press.

Bourguignon, E. (1979). *A world of women: Anthropological studies of women in the societies of the world.* New York: Praeger.

Canino, G. (1982a). The Hispanic woman: Sociocultural influences on diagnoses and treatment. In R. Becerra, M. Karno, & J. Escobar (Eds.) *Mental health and Hispanic Americans* (pp. 117-138). New York: Grune and Stratton.

Canino, G. (1982b). Transactional family patterns: A preliminary exploration of Puerto Rican female adolescents. In R. E. Zambrana (Ed.) *Work, family and health: Latina women in transition* (pp. 27-36). New York: Hispanic Research Center, Fordham University.

Comas-Díaz, L. (1982). Mental health needs of mainland Puerto Rican women. In R. E. Zambrana (Ed.) *Work, family and health: Latina women in transition* (pp. 1-10). New York: Hispanic Research Center, Fordham University.

Comas-Díaz, L., Geller, J.D., Melgoza, B., & Baker, R. (1982, August). *Atti-*

tudes and expectations about mental health services among Hispanics and Afro-Americans. Paper presented at the 90th Annual Convention of the American Psychological Association, Washington, D.C.

Costello, R. (1977). "Chicana liberation" and the Mexican American marriage. *Psychiatric Annals, 7*(12), 52-63.

De La Cancela, V. (1986). A critical analysis of Puerto Rican machismo: Implications for clinical practice. *Psychotherapy, 2*(2), 291-296.

Dill, B.T. (1983, Spring). Race, class and gender: Prospects for an all-inclusive sisterhood. *Feminist Studies, 9*(1), 132-150.

Douglas, M.A. & Walker, L. (Eds.) (in press). *Feminist psychotherapies: Integration of therapeutic and feminist systems*. New York: Ablex Publishing Corporation.

Espin, O.M. (1984, August). *Selection of Hispanic female healers in urban U.S. communities*. Paper presented at the American Psychological Association Meeting, Toronto, Canada.

Espin, O.M. (1985). Psychotherapy with Hispanic women: Some considerations. In P. Pedersen (Ed.) *Handbook of cross-cultural counseling and therapy* (pp. 165-171). Westport, Connecticut: Greenwood Press.

Espin, O.M. (1986). Cultural and historical influences on sexuality in Hispanic/Latin women. In J. Cole (Ed.) *All American women* (pp. 272-284). New York: Free Press.

Falicov, C.J. (1982). Mexican families. In M. McGoldrick, J.K. Pearce, & J. Giordano (Eds.) *Ethnicity and family therapy* (pp. 134-163). New York: The Guilford Press.

Fernández-Méndez, E. (1972). *Art and mythology of the Taíno Indians of the Greater West Indies*. San Juan: Ediciones El Cemí.

Giraldo, D. (1972). El machismo como fenómeno psicocultural. (Machismo as a psychocultural phenomenon.) *Revista Latino-Americana de Psicología, 4*(3), 295-309.

Greeley, A.M. (1981). *The Irish Americans*. New York: Harper & Row.

Gómez, A.M. (1982). Puerto Rican Americans. In A. Gaw (Ed.) *Cross-cultural psychiatry* (pp. 109-136). Littleton, Massachusetts: John Wright.

Habach, E. (1972). *Ni machismo, ni hembrismo*. (Neither *machismo* nor *hembrismo*). Colección: Protesta. Caracas: Publicaciones EPLA.

Hidalgo, H.A., & Christensen, E.H. (1976-77, Winter). The Puerto Rican lesbian and the Puerto Rican community. *Journal of Homosexuality, 2*(2), 109-121.

Hynes, K., & Werbin, J. (1977). Group psychotherapy for Spanish-speaking women. *Psychiatric Annals, 7*(12), 52-63.

Kinzer, N. (1973). Women in Latin America: Priests, machos, and babies, or Latin American women and the Manichean heresy. *Journal of Marriage and the Family, 35*, 299-312.

Klerman, G.L., Weissman, M.M., Rounsaville, B.J., & Chevron, E.S. (1984). *Interpersonal psychotherapy of depression*. New York: Basic Books, Inc. Publishers.

López-Garriga, M. (1978). Estrategias de autoafirmación en mujeres puertorriqueñas (Strategies of self affirmation among Puerto Rican women). *Revista de Ciencias Sociales, 20*, 259-267.

Maduro, R. (1983, December). Curanderismo and Latino views of disease and curing. *The Western Journal of Medicine, 139*(6), 868-874.

Mays, V., & Comas-Díaz, L. (in press). Feminist therapy with ethnic minority populations: A closer look at Blacks and Hispanics. In M.A. Douglas & L.E. Walker (eds.) *Feminist psychotherapies: Integration of therapeutic and feminist systems.* New York: Ablex Publishing Corporation.

Padilla, A.M., & Ruiz, R. (1973). *Latino mental health: A review of literature.* Rockville, MD: National Institute of Mental Health.

San Martin, H. (1975). Machismo: Latin America's myth-cult of male supremacy. *il por UNESCO Courier, 28*, 28-32.

Senour, M.N. (1977). Psychology of the Chicana. In J.L. Martinez (Ed.) *Chicano psychology* (pp. 329-342). New York: Academic Press.

Sluski, C.E. (1979). Migration and family conflict. *Family Process, 18*(4), 379-390.

Sluski, C.E. (1982). The Latin lover revisited. In M. McGoldrick, J.K. Pearce, & J. Giordano (Eds.) *Ethnicity and family therapy* (pp. 492-498). New York: The Pergamon Press.

Steiner, S. (1974). *The islands: The worlds of the Puerto Ricans.* New York: Harper Colophon Books.

Stevens, E. (1973). Machismo and marianismo. *Transaction-Society, 10*(6), 57-63.

Takooshian, H.A. & Stuart, C.R. (1983). Ethnicity and feminism among American women: Opposing social trends? *International Journal of Group Tensions, 13*(1-4), 100-105.

Torres-Matrullo, C. (1980). Acculturation, sex-role values and mental health among Puerto Ricans in the mainland United States. In A.M. Padilla (Ed.). *Acculturation: Theory, models and some new findings* (pp. 120-132). Boulder: Westview Press.

Zayas, N., & Silen, J. (1972). *La mujer en la lucha de hoy* (the woman in today's struggle). San Juan, Puerto Rico: Ediciones Ki Kiri Kí.

The Impostor

I am a mother
although I have
this nightmare
that one of these days
someone will ask
to see my credentials.

I am a mother of two
although sometimes
they look at me
accusingly
because there are not enough hours
in my day.

I am a mother
although for the life of me
I don't know how to handle
their fits
much less mine.

I am a mother
who still needs mothering
and sometimes resents her mother
because she has to mother my father.

I am a fatherless mother
who has to wear two hats

Suzana Cabañas was born in Puerto Rico and raised in Brooklyn, New York. Her work has appeared in numerous publications including *En Rojo/Claridad, Third World Women, Breaking,* and *Third Woman.* Author of one published collection of poetry, *Poemario,* she lives and works in New York where she is actively involved in the Puerto Rican independence movement.

"The Imposter" appeared in *Heresies.* It is reprinted here with permission of the author and *Heresies.*

but never quite knows when
to wear which one.

I am a mother
who doesn't know how she got here
and sometimes
thank god it's only sometimes
wishes she could resign.

Suzana Cabañas

The Necessary Bitch

Judy Simmons

Sometimes I act like a bitch for the same reasons that Sojourner Truth ripped off her bodice in public and asked, "Ain't I a woman too?" I mean, really, am I not somebody's child? Don't I bleed if you cut me? Haven't I dreamed of flying?

When people treat me as if the answer to those questions is "No," I feel chumped off, choked up, unloved, frustrated and angry. For most of my life I handled those feelings by crawling alone into a dark corner and crying. I had been strictly taught to be a docile Negro, a proper Lady and a turn-the-other-cheek Christian. I had taken the lessons to heart. Negroes knew they'd be lynched if they stood up for themselves. Ladies didn't even learn the vocabulary of cussing somebody out and would rather have died than be involved in a confrontation or "scene." Christians of the variety I was trained to be left vengeance to the Lord, comforting themselves with the conviction that on Judgment Day their tormentors would go to hell.

All that's well and good as far as it goes, but it doesn't go very far in the capitalistic, post-1950s, urban world I live in. I suspect that if Frederick Douglass, Harriet Tubman, Sojourner and a host of less-legendary Black folk had bent their backs under such ideas, cotton would still be king and we'd be fully employed—as slaves in perpetuity.

Yet when a woman, and certainly a Black woman, won't act like

Judy Simmons is a poet, broadcast and print journalist, and lecturer living in Mount Vernon, NY. Her most recent volume of poems is *Decent Intentions*, Blind Begger Press, Bronx, NY.

a Negro, a Lady and a martyr Christian, she usually gets labeled a bitch. A woman is a bitch if she stands up for herself, speaks her mind, insists on her rights and space, isn't deferential to men and would rather make a scene than die or turn the other cheek. Except if she's over 65 *and* a grandmother: Then asserting herself is okay because she's already sacrificed herself for home, hubby, kids, church and community, so she deserves a little indulgence. Besides, she's no threat. Her physical powers are waning, she's no longer a sex object and she's usually not still competing for position and power.

A younger woman who doesn't make the million compromises that being "feminine" requires is likely to be seen as a bitch (and a closet butch) by most men and many women. However, this may be more true for people over 35 than for those born during and after the 1960s.

Women have managed to bend the bars of the femininity jail in the last 20 years, so that a bit more of their (or their daughters') individuality can escape. I imagine that no 20-year-old woman today has had to fight about whether or not pants are appropriate attire. I pray that no woman under 30 has had the experience of wearing a rubber (*all* rubber) Playtex girdle in 95° summer weather (just remembering doing that makes me evil with the whole world). Probably somebody somewhere still teaches girls that feminine women never develop full voices and go to their graves sounding like whining children or a Mississippi Miss America. These sorts of things made my young life miserable. They knocked me out of contention for power positions by keeping me focused on trivial matters. My resentment at being miseducated and wasted in these ways contributes to the uncompromising attitudes and sometimes tactless action that get me tagged as a bitch. And this is just the light stuff.

Last year a Black man nearing 30 with whom I frequently talked said that Black women have an attitude he doesn't like. He told me this several times, usually when he had to go through a Black woman to get something he needed — such as a credit-union loan — or when the superficial charm he turned on didn't get him so much as a raised eyebrow (the man has a greedy ego). I asked him what this attitude he detected only in Black women was all about. My understanding of his reply is that Black women don't give up the light pleasantries that let him get his foot in the door with some white — and especially European — women. Black women — the ones he generalizes about — are suspicious, hostile or simply indifferent to people and situations that don't directly concern their own business. In other words, Black women are evil Black bitches.

Finally, this man succeeded in provoking the evil Black bitch out of *me* with his insistence on this stereotype. After trying unsuccessfully to reason with him about the triple eight-balls Black women live behind, I just told him he had no right to an opinion on the subject because he'd lived a very sheltered life, had never walked one step in a Black woman's moccasins and, besides, didn't like his mother or treat her well. The pictures that flashed through my mind's angry eye as I told him this hurt me to my heart.

I saw Black women bent double for 12 hours a day, eight-foot sacks harnessed to their backs, picking cotton with cracked, bloody fingers. *In 1955.* One of them was my college-graduate mother, who wasn't paid enough as a Negro teacher in the segregated South to feed, clothe and shelter only the two of us.

I saw my dark-skinned, country roommate at Talladega College who kept her eyes on the floor and meekly submitted to bullying because that's what a black Black girl with nappy hair could expect and deserved. *In 1960.*

I saw the women of Laurel, Mississippi, whose work in a chicken factory gave them bloated, ulcerated arms, and who bled through to their outer garments because they'd be fired if they left the line to change their menstrual pad or tampon. *In 1980.* (See "Southern Shame: Local 882 on the Line" by Rosemary L. Bray, *Essence*, March 1981.)

I saw the apparently endless stream of urban Black girls born into the welfare cycle who have no place to be somebody and no one to teach them how. In her book *Pathways to Work*, labor economist Dr. Phyllis Wallace shows how racism, classism and sexism combine to prevent most of these girls from making the education and work connections that would lead them out of poverty and deprivation. Thinking of these vulnerable girls and women made me detest the guy I was talking with. As Mr. Smalltown Bourgeois, he has specialized in sexually and emotionally exploiting his social inferiors, whom he could not *possibly* be expected to marry—but rather than 'fessing up to his purely doggish intentions, he says he's "helping them realize their potential" (by letting them touch the hem of his, uh, garment) and "saving" them from the real brutes who would physically beat them. No wonder he's contemptuous of Black women. They've been his victims, "the slave of the slave, the mule of the world" as Zora Neale Hurston said in her novel *Their Eyes Were Watching God*. If being able to see through the likes of him and draw blood in the clinches makes a woman a bitch, we need a lot more of them, and I'll be glad to be counted as one.

It wasn't always so.

In 1973—after *not* going off on (a) the Black man I was going with; (b) the white men I worked with; (c) the multiracial women who drilled all that docility into me and (d) my shrink, who was crazier than his patients—I cut both my wrists with a razor blade. I wasn't trying to kill myself. But I had sat on my pain, grief and rage for too long—I was so mad, in every sense of the word, that I had to draw blood; and I told myself that if it were my own blood I wouldn't wind up in jail. The next morning I walked over to St. Vincent's Hospital, in Greenwich Village in New York City. While my left wrist was being stitched I decided that something was definitely wrong with responding to others' hurting me by hurting myself more. So I went looking for my bitch.

Not that I knew it was a bitch I needed. I was seeking mental health, social adjustment, mature realism, self-actualization, empowerment and all the other psychobabble concepts. Twelve years later, I can see all that meant I was looking for my bitch. And I found her. And I'm happy to have her on my side.

Well, I'm happy about having a strong, protective part of me taking care of business, but I'm not comfortable thinking of myself as a bitch. When I was growing up, it was a very bad word used only by low-class people who drank, fornicated, cut each other up on Saturday night and had daughters who disgraced them by having babies out of wedlock. It was a deadly insult even among these people living under Booker T.'s "veil of ignorance." "Don't be callin' me no bitch!" was usually the last spoken sound you heard before two girls went to blows in a rural Alabama schoolyard.

For me—the only daughter, niece and grandbaby of Alabama

schoolteachers, and the offspring of the unfortunate marriage between that "poor southern girl" and the eldest son of genteel Rhode Island strivers with aristocratic pretensions—using profane language of any kind was a mortal and severely punishable offense. Joan, my friend who counsels at Bronx Community College, grew up under the same prohibition. Her minister father made it clear that the word was profane and the concept disgusting. It referred to a loose woman who had sex without benefit of marriage and was vain and worldly—a gaudy, painted harlot who probably sang "Gimme mah gin!" and wiggled her hips, tempting upright, God-fearing men to stray from the straight and narrow. Virtuous girls had to avoid even the appearance of evil by keeping their legs crossed, their eyes downcast, their mouths full of soap and their heads clouded with fear and guilt for having sinful thoughts.

Sinful thoughts included sexual ones, of course, but those were venial compared with an even worse heresy: thinking that you, a mere female, were as good as or even better than boys and men. This was a truly unthinkable thought, so I didn't think it. Instead I became schizoid, in the popular sense of the word. On one level I believed that boys and men were the Father-Gods whose love and approval I desperately needed to save me from unnamed evils. On another level I was determined to prove that anything a boy could do, I could do better. I'd be a nuclear physicist, a master psychologist, a captain of industry. At the very least I'd marry a white man and be the power behind the throne. Even being a mistress attracted me, because she got to have love, sex and wealth without the drudgery of children, housekeeping and having the guy around all the time lording over her.

Obviously my schizophrenia (loosely speaking) stems from my conflicting reactions to sexism and racism (all mixed up with fundamentalist Christianity and Victorian mores). To attract and keep Father-God men, I have to be feminine, which means being short, slim, blonde, blue-eyed, domesticated but stylish, and either stupid or deceitful so they will always feel they have the upper hand. I'm neither physically nor temperamentally suited to the part. I'm five feet eight inches tall, weigh 180 pounds and am black-haired, brown-eyed, ferociously intelligent, kinda wild and determined to run as much of my life and the world as I can get under my control. Conflict.

To be Black and marginally comfortable, I have to accept gradual change of the oppressive status quo; act dumb enough not to threaten white people, but appear intelligent enough to be useful and worthy of their liberal investment; plus I have to come to terms with never getting the opportunities, status, respect and wealth received by whites who are my peers in terms of initiative, ability and achievement. I'm not suited to this part either. I have little patience, hate injustice against anyone, resent taking crumbs when I've earned a whole loaf, and certainly don't believe in passive resistance, though I've practiced it to keep my butt intact and out of jail. More conflict!

The conflict isn't only between me and outsiders — it's inside me, which makes things harder. My feeling about the word *bitch* is an example of my internal conflicts: Like my friend Dawn, a film director who lives in Minneapolis, I'm sometimes flattered when people call me a bitch. It means they're acknowledging my strength, my ability to back them up and make them respect me. Yet I also feel that the word *bitch* is like the word *nigger*. You can use it familiarly, colloquially or even affectionately among friends, but it still has disparaging echoes and images attached to it. Thinking myself a bitch makes me feel something ugly and mean inside. It's as if the image I have of myself being assertive is that of a vicious dog, with bared fangs dripping foam.

I think we're cheating ourselves by accepting the bitch label and trying to make it mean something positive. We're having enough trouble gaining self-esteem as it is, without using a very suspect word to label the kind of person we're struggling to become. *Bitch* is too easy and narrow a concept for what's really going on with me, with us women.

Since the mid-1960s many, maybe most, of us have been expressing feminism in our lives, whether or not we recognize it and call it that. Many Black women are unwilling to identify with feminism, apparently feeling that a feminist is a privileged white, racist, anti-male woman. In fact, *feminist* means exactly what some of us are trying to make *bitch* mean: a woman who takes her power out of others' hands and into her own and decides who she wants to be, how she'll be responsible and what she'll make of life on her own terms.

In one way, Black women have a head start on this: We have long had a high degree of responsibility, decision-making power and self-reliance in family and social matters. However, I think many of us have neither sought nor enjoyed our independence. We wanted and expected to be part of the romantic nuclear family, despite all the evidence we've had for generations that this is a slim possibility. So we've tended to feel cheated and mistreated by men and life. Since we don't realistically prepare ourselves for the responsibilities that remain after our dependent-mating dreams die, we're usually under the gun financially and psychologically—overwhelmed, overburdened and feeling powerless.

Frequently those of us who do pick up on some of feminism's flashier aspects make the fundamental mistake of wanting the privilege without paying the price. Taking power and directing our lives isn't simply a matter of flexing our women's-lib mouth muscles and throwing jargonistic tantrums to get our own way. One bright woman in her mid-twenties with a lovely two-year-old son told me two years ago that she had to pursue personal growth and self-discovery, so she was thinking of leaving her husband and giving him custody of their child. Further conversation revealed that her marriage wasn't bad—just not exciting; mostly she felt she was missing out on the wonderful freedoms of the single new woman. Hah!

I suggested to her that marriage and motherhood were choices she had already made as part of her personal growth and self-discovery. Indeed, she had grown and discovered enough of herself to want now to change the way she functioned in the marriage and to branch out in other ways as well. Counseling her not to throw the baby out with the bathwater, I reminded her that accepting responsibility for the consequences of one's choices and commitments is the basis of personal growth; and that even if she felt her choice of marriage and family had been made just to go along with the social program, she must have had a personal need to do that or else she could have been like me, never married, twice pregnant and twice aborted.

A couple of months ago this woman sought me out, handed me a luxuriant bouquet of flowers and said that thanks to me, she and her husband have been working together successfully to accommodate her changed perception of herself. She's developing separate career interests and broader skills too, and her child still has two cohabiting parents. This woman may choose not to be married someday, but at least the choice will be based on something more substantial than temporary "bitchiness," half-baked notions of feminism and the old feeling of the grass being greener elsewhere.

Being a new-style bitch or a feminist isn't just a matter of waking up one morning and shouting "I gotta be me." I've been doing that for years, and all it makes me is a rebellious child who has spent her life *reacting against* other people instead of *moving toward* her own identity and goals. All I know is that I don't want to be a schoolteacher or a pillar of the church. I don't want any man to get away with seeing me and 15 other women. I don't want to accept the role that a nigger bitch is given in this society. I don't want to work at some job I don't like so I can get a pension. And I don't want any more girls to grow up thinking that the best they can do with their lives is spread their legs to let in a man and let out a baby.

When people start pushing on me with things I don't want, I get upset and eventually start pushing back. But since I'm operating off negatives instead of positives, I've usually let things go on too long before deciding I can't take it, I've had enough. Which means that my response may not be very nice or rational, and I can understand why someone on the receiving end of my rebellion may think I'm a nasty bitch. I bring out the big guns and go for the jugular and don't give a damn about the relationship, the job or whatever. I just want release and relief. That's why I was able to counsel that woman about running away from her marriage: I've gone to extremes often enough myself to know how much you lose that way. By the time I decide to put a stop to what's bugging me, I've usually slipped so far down in my own eyes that I need revenge to restore my self-respect. The sad thing about this is that every situation or relationship represents an investment, and when you blow it all up in a rage — no matter how justified — you don't give yourself the opportunity to collect any dividends, even if they're down the line and not what, or as much as, you initially expected. It's the old maxim about not burning bridges.

If I were a feminist instead of a bitch, I would have identified, for example, what behavior I can accept from a lover and what I can't. So the first or second time he didn't make it over when he said he would and called me two days later with some lame line, I'd make my limits clear and remove him from my life, or at least my bed, the very next time he did it. Instead, what I've usually done is tell myself I love him, I need him, he's confused and deserves my special understanding, blah, blah. So I've kept dealing and being disappointed and going for the okeydoke and getting more involved, and also more resentful. Finally, I decide I'm being a real jerk and go off. By then I'm badly hurt and he's bewildered, 'cause he's doing what he was always doing, and all he can say is, "What's wrong with the bitch? What *do* she want?"

I want to stop being my own worst enemy and start being my best friend. I want to decide who I am, mostly, and what work I want to do, seriously. I want to spend half as much energy and ingenuity making myself economically and politically powerful as I've spent trying to show some man how worthwhile my love, loyalty and talents are to him (I'll be filthy rich in six months). I want women and men to respect their separate-but-equal struggles to be whole, balanced human beings. And when I'm standing up for myself and my beliefs to the best of my ability, I want to be recognized as a complex, loving, hurting, angry, courageous woman. Maybe a feminist. Definitely much more and *much better* than a bitch.

"Conscious Subjectivity" or Use of One's Self in Therapeutic Process

Virginia W. Hammond

To work most effectively with women, one must have clear understanding of the course and consequences of the socialization process of women in this culture. The specifics of one's economic status, class and ethnicity will of course personalize and individualize the context of these socialization experiences for each woman. However, the prevailing self-limiting and negative impact of sexism on the psychological, emotional and social development of women is a societal reality, not to be escaped by any female reared, educated and acculturated in this culture (Epstein, 1970).

As a Black therapist, I have not only experienced the burdens of sexism, but have had to struggle to achieve some degree of self-actualization and self-power in spite of the oppressive forces of both sexism and racism. As I struggle to continue my growth and development as a Black and female clinician, I have also become increasingly aware of the value of certain life experiences and their potency for application in both my personal and professional life.

I have come to identify this heightened self-awareness as a "conscious subjectivity." Conscious subjectivity refers to the framework and attitude I consciously bring to the therapeutic encounter.

Virginia W. Hammond, MEd, is a licensed clinical psychologist and certified school psychologist. Currently the Director of Child and Family Outpatient Services of the Hall Mercer Community Mental Health/Mental Retardation Center of Pennsylvania Hospital in Philadelphia, Virginia Hammond also has a private practice in family and individual psychotherapy. She has led workshops on emotional problems of children, the development of Black adolescents, depression in Black women, stress management, and family therapy.

My development of an increased sense of self and heightened appreciation of my own potentialities has facilitated both a personal and professional empowerment.

In reflecting upon the course my own consciousness raising journey and the subsequent development of a personalized "theory," I chart several events in my life as catalysts for these changes and growth. After many years of working as a child psychologist and family therapist, I began to supervise psychology interns. This new role as a precepter for students training to be family therapists brought into sharp contrast the difference between what I said and believed one *should* do as a therapist and what I actually saw myself do as a therapist (via videotapes). For a period of time, I struggled to bring these two images into harmony by consciously striving to demonstrate and teach the students only those therapeutic behaviors compatible and consistent with the theory in which I had been trained. The dissonance I experienced during this phase of my professional life was significant and no doubt contributed to my need to seek out and establish alliances with other Black professionals. For the first time in my professional life I began sharing ideas, collaborating almost exclusively with other Black clinicians and corroborating with them my own clinical experiences. It was as if my mentoring, which heretofore had been provided by representatives of the "establishment," was now being conducted by my consciousness raising group. The interminable post-session dialogues we held not only forced me to confront the contradictions within my work, but the group also provided the necessary support and validation which would allow me to begin work as a therapist in a more egosyntonic, and therefore more effective, manner. With this perspective, I can be a prominent tool to be used strategically in the process of psychotherapy. I am very much aware of the controversial nature of this expressed attitude and approach, especially in view of the teaching, doctrine and constructs of traditional psychiatric and psychotherapeutic approaches. I will counter such criticism only by saying that the traditional theories, and consequently the emergent treatment approaches, reflect blatant sexist attitudes, prejudices and generally negative valuation of female qualities (cf. Freud, 1933). I see no justification or need to perpetuate this orientation (theoretical or applied) in my work with women.

The consciousness raising process propelled me to the re-assessment of my role in the therapeutic process. This personal evaluation led me quite naturally from level one—increased self-awareness (conscious subjectivity) to level two—the concept of empowerment. "Empowerment" in its broadest and most fundamental form is being acutely and perceptively aware of one's self (competence, skills, knowledge, deficits, etc.) and having the capacity to apply this knowledge to achieve desired ends. Empowering concepts are the outgrowth of the "knowledge skills" model presented by McClelland (1975), and are a legitimate goal of therapy with all clients. I further contend that women and other cultural minority group members can be treated successfully *only* within the framework of an empowerment model.

Currently, most of the clients I see in therapy are women, many of whom have entered therapy because of problems such as depression, abuse and family problems. These problems are often directly related to the effects of sexism and/or racism. Specifically, many of the women are under-educated, under-employed and living in oppressed or oppressive conditions. The therapeutic alliance provides the mechanism to foster and develop a sense of empowerment in these clients, that is, to facilitate the belief and action necessary to place one in the center of one's own life. Pinderhughes (1982) defines the empowerment concept as "the capacity to influence for one's own benefit the forces which affect one's life space."

Central to the concept of empowerment is the ability and the capacity to use one's self, to create options for one's self and, most importantly, to reject the ideology of powerlessness and personal inadequacy (Pinderhughes & Pittman, 1985) that constrains us. Consistent with this objective, I believe it is imperative that the therapist or "helping professional" demonstrate the model and the ability to use one's self in the therapeutic process in the service of empowering the client. Some of the procedures and strategies I have used to achieve this goal include the following.

Mutual Identification Points

This strategy involves owning and expressing common or shared experiences with the client. This approach allows therapist and client to identify and use in therapy similarities in our collective experiences as women. Use of this strategy facilitates joining, provides for ongoing role analysis and clarification of the therapeutic relationship responsibilities of both the client and the therapist. As a Black and female therapist, I have experienced the negative impact of sexism, racism and oppression. These experiences have enhanced my force as a therapist because I not only can validate the client's perception that these obstacles exist, but can serve to model an example of survival. Based on the concept of mutual identification, I directly challenge statements my clients make which suggest my lack of resemblance to them (e.g., "You don't know what it feels like to be depressed"). I counter by sharing some of my history to correct or modify such misperceptions.

Psychological research has consistently shown that mutuality (e.g., experience, education, social class, ethnicity, etc.) between client and therapist correlates positively with many variables measuring successful outcome of treatment. Could this finding be the outcome of or related to the benefit of the mutual or shared identification process between therapist and client?

Power Agent

To be truly supportive to the client, the therapist not only must work to influence the therapeutic encounter, but must also seize each and every opportunity to influence other relevant systems in which the client participates as a member of society. For example, the therapist's work as a power agent may be simply making a telephone call on the client's behalf, or it may be as complex and challenging as mounting appeals to secure denied benefits or services. The role of the power agent certainly includes advocating for the client whenever possible. In my role as a power agent, letters of recommendation have been written, legal testimony given, recitals attended, and interagency meetings attended as I functioned as an advocate for my clients.

Validation of Strength

This is a tremendously important area to attend to because more often than not, the victimized, impoverished and discouraged do not reflect a concept of self which recognizes their strengths. Consequently, I consciously set out to insure that each therapeutic encounter includes identification and the relabeling of behavior to indicate the existence of strength or competency in my clients. To emphasize the individual strength, power and ability of a particular client, I will request that she maintain a journal listing all of the activities she completed between sessions. Negative self-evaluative statements are explored to uncover distortions, and corrective self-identifying statements are practiced. Take, for example, an unemployed mother of four, who, whenever she was questioned regarding some accomplishment of hers, would reply, "I just did what had to be done." Obviously, she was accustomed to minimizing her abilities and skills of resourcefulness. Self-deprecating statements (attitudes) are challenged and explored. Validation of strength fosters a positive view of self.

Self-Disclosures

This strategy reflects a non-traditional view of the client-therapist relationship and is a rejection of the principle of the therapist's non-self-disclosure. I feel that the therapist's ability to demonstrate and model the desired behavior has a very positive effect on the therapeutic relationship and is a critical factor in an empowerment therapy. Timely and appropriate self-disclosing behavior can also be viewed as an example of skill teaching which is another important use of one's self in therapy. One client, a young woman who had put all her hopes for a better life in her young son and was devastated when told he was learning disabled, told me how enlightening and empowering it was for her when I shared that I had been through an extended school placement problem with my own son, a situation very similar to the one she was currently caught up in at her child's school. Several therapy sessions were devoted to reviewing the particular school law and strategizing a course of action to secure appropriate placement for her child.

Skill Teaching

I am currently "teaching" a client how to strategize to be a viable candidate for an anticipated promotion opportunity in her corporation. The use of myself in the process of empowering my clients allows me to act on my commitment to foster self-reliance, mastery and competency in my clients. This is often achieved through specific teaching of skills. Skill teaching with my clients has included the following: teaching child management techniques, assertive behavior, relaxation exercises, support group organization, and resumé writing. Psychological welfare is not possible without the necessary skills needed to negotiate within one's environment. The therapist's view of self must include the responsibility for specific skill development of the client as well as for improving psychological functioning.

The additional strategies just outlined are used in a conscious and deliberate fashion and contribute to my functioning as a role model for the clients with whom I work. The empowerment treatment model requires the therapist to model openness, the capacity to feel, the ability to be action-oriented, and the reorganization of self-identity from victimization to empowerment.

What is the impact of "conscious subjectivity" on both the clients who have been exposed to this approach and my own development as a psychotherapist? While I have not conducted any formal studies to evaluate the outcome of my therapeutic approach, my own experience as well as subjective reports received from clients would suggest that this approach is a suitable match for many of the women with whom I worked. How my former and current clients are living their lives indicates that it has been helpful; many of the women achieve an increased sense of control and direction over their lives. As for my own development as a Black female clinician, the process of developing and practicing "conscious subjectivity" has had significant impact. I feel confident about my work, my ability to be productive and effective with clients, especially Black women, and to use myself as a tool for their empowerment. It is, I believe, enormously respectful of who they are. My journey, and theirs, will continue.

REFERENCES

Bond, G., & Lieberman, M. (1980). The role and function of women's consciousness raising. In C. Heckerman (Ed.), *The evolving female*. New York: Human Sciences Press.

Epstein, F.F. (1970). *Women's place*. Berkeley: University of California Press.

Freud, S. (1933). *New introductory letters on psychoanalysis*. New York: W.W. Norton.

McClelland, D. (1975). Power: The inner experience. New York: Wiley and Sons.

Pinderhughes, E. (1982). *Empowerment for our clients and for ourselves*. Unpublished manuscript.

Pinderhughes, E., & Pittman, A. (1985). Socio-cultural treatment model of empowerment of worker and client. In M. Day (Ed.), *The socio-cultural dimensions of mental health*. New York: Vantage Press.

Smith, A., & Stewart, A. (1983). Racism and sexism in black women's lives. *Journal of Social Issues, 39* (3).

Zucker, H. (1967). *Problems of psychotherapy*. New York: The Free Press.

First Dialogue

(With our comrades, who daily . . .)
    "In that way, put an end to the
    old non-communist psychology."
                                    V.I. Lenin
                        (On women's role in society,
                        from Clara Zetkin's notebooks)

Here comes my secular skirt again
    and Anguish circles my throat.
These breasts that calmed my daughters' cries
move together, rise, stand up
and strike for the milk of life.

Then I blame myself—old habit—
for my white hands, the head scarves, lipstick, purse,
those nine months dawning,
and fail to understand the root,
                        the seed,
                        the flower.

Where are you: manspirit of my time,
every afternoon home from work
become exactly that fountain of rude stares
    reproaching me the quick lunch,
    pile of unwashed clothes,
    handkerchiefs not perfectly ironed.
This daily existence.

So often I see you
red card proud in the pocket of your shirt,

Milagros González is a poet and police-woman in Cuba's Isle of Youth.
"First Dialogue" appeared in *Women of Cuba: Twenty Years Later* by Marga-
ret Randall. It is reprinted with the permission of Smyrna Press, Box 1803-GPO,
Brooklyn, NY 11202.

83

your honors,
your medals
your gun,
your work: humble *Homeland or Death* of every day
breaking between your hands
where callouses, shovels, papers, all of you move on
   without reproach,
   without protest,
   without a word.

The draining fear comes over me when I meet your wonder
at the rag I hand you
to help dismiss the dust:
that weariness, you don't know how, the newspaper, so tired,
that meeting or what's worse sometimes:
it's just not what you've got planned for today.

Then I remind you of Luis, Pedro, Juan,
the guy across the street
or next door. Nothing.
You're not good at shopping. And your name isn't Juan.

Man to whom I give my root, my belly, my mind,
my small joy divided among these ragged socks, unsewn
when you need to dress well . . .
What difference to you
that the children make their beds
pick up their shoes
and help me dry the dishes
if you study for your next class
in the most comfortable chair we have
and keep your fear in shadow, almost hidden
so no one will discover that *macho* at the base of your spine!
And you make Revolution from the Five Year Plan
but as you can, straddling Rocinante
while Dulcinea admires your prowess, the lance, the windmills,
and you, in the neighborhood, defending the social advantages
of our new Constitution!
     You make Revolution:

starched shirt,
clean refrigerator,
beds made,
shining pots,
floors so clean you can eat or spit on them.

Well, no.

Go, search for yourself at the root. Grow.
No longer does everyone follow you.
The men of your time are of another breed,
    jump time and space.
Don't forget it when shame comes up
to plant the hypocrite kiss on your brow
and you run and hide the mop — company's come —
surprised at your own conditioning, comrade.

Now that your specialty
is breaking your balls for Future,
keep in mind
we're neither distance nor different lands,
winds of the same new world we are, reborn,
we're all October!
Learn then to heat your food while I study,
put your diplomas away,
all that coursework with honors,
take down the titles: doctor,
                    engineer
                    journalist
                    sailor
and — why not? — technician in loneliness,
    architect of anguish.

Because Revolution is more than I want,
                    more than Party member,
                    more than Congress, Assembly
your eyelids closing over the book, the seed,
gun raised, fraternal death.

REVOLUTION
is also we who make and do
who plough with you,
who pencil, who trench . . .
Revolution is your hands once more
your warm voice when I'm tired,
you, seated next to my blood
as I wash the dishes
and the smile when duty calls
and we share the task of leaving our bed.

Revolution, my love, will also be
when day breaks one of these centuries
and pride strokes the militant home,
the honey in your hands turned sweet again.

Comrade, when the day breaks,
you'll have risen, finally,
TO THE HIGHEST HUMAN PLANE.

Milagros Gonzáles

Marxism, Psychoanalysis and Feminism:
A View from Latin America

Nancy Caro Hollander

In the initial stages of the contemporary women's liberation movement in the United States and Europe, feminists often theoretically and politically opposed Marxism because of its relegation of women's struggles to a secondary position relative to class struggle and condemned psychoanalysis because of its conceptual and clinical adaptation of women to the existing gendered arrangements of male-dominated society.

However, in the ongoing dialogue between feminists and Marxists, new theories and political strategies have arisen which provide a critical analysis of class and gender as two mutually reinforcing systems oppressive to women. And in recent years, an important current has emerged within feminist thought which appropriates certain aspects of psychoanalysis in order to develop a theory of the subjectivity of gender inequality and to analyze the acquisition of gender identity and the unconscious mechanisms by which the ideology and institutions of the existing gendered order are reproduced.

Nancy Caro Hollander, PhD, teaches Latin American History and Women's Studies at California State University, Dominguez Hills. She is also training in a post-doctoral program as a research psychoanalyst. She produces and hosts a one hour, biweekly radio program on Pacifica Radio.

The information in this article comes from research on Marie Langer's life and work which forms the basis of a biography in progress. Over the past three years, the author has spent many weeks with Langer in Mexico, taping almost 60 hours of interviews with her. In June, 1984, the author traveled to Nicaragua with Langer to observe the work of the Internationalist Team of Mental Health Workers. This research has been partially funded by the Plumsock Fund.

87

Latin America provides us with an important precursor to this intersection of Marxism, psychoanalysis and feminism in the conceptualization of female oppression and the fetters, external and internal, to change. Marie Langer, a 77-year-old Austrian-born Argentine psychoanalyst, has spent the past five decades integrating her professional expertise with a political commitment to a Marxist and feminist vision of a humane social order. Langer's political activism and her contributions to a psychoanalytic understanding of women are well known throughout Latin America and much of Europe. This article will introduce Langer to North Americans, focusing on her interest in the psychological and social conflicts inherent in women's particular location within the class/gender system. First, however, a brief overview of her life will help to contextualize our discussion.

MARIE LANGER: A LIFE OF COMMITMENT

Langer was born in 1910, the second of two daughters, to a rich and progressive Jewish family in Vienna, Austria. Her youth was spent in the exciting politicized culture of "Red Vienna," ruled by the world's only mass based Social Democratic Party. She had the privilege of attending the famous Schwerzwald Schule, where Marxist and feminist instructors formally introduced Langer to a critical vision of the world and provided alternative role models to the stifling life style expected of women of her social class. Langer chose to study medicine, and in the early thirties, following graduation from medical school, she began training in Freud's renowned Wiener Vereinigung Institut. There she studied with the well known female psychoanalysts, Helene Deutsch and Jeanne Lampl de Groot. However, this period, dominated by the rise to power of Fascism, was to be a fateful turning point in Langer's life. She became active in the clandestine leftist opposition within Austria, and like many of her intellectual and political counterparts, went to Spain, where as a physician on the battlefields, she cared for soldiers wounded in the defense of the Spanish Republic.

After the victory of Franco's fascist forces, Langer was forced to flee Europe because of anti-semitism and anti-communism. She and her husband emigrated to Uruguay, and after several very difficult years, settled in Buenos Aires, Argentina in the early forties. There she would develop a professional identity as the most prominent female psychoanalyst in Latin America and a political reputation as a vocal advocate of political justice in the Latin American struggles against neo-colonialism and repressive military dictatorships. Because of her leadership role during the late 1960s and early 1970s in the radicalization of the mental health community and her outspoken denunciation of the human rights violations of the repressive governments of Argentina during that time, Langer experienced the second forced uprooting of her life: in 1974, she was targeted for assassination by one of Argentina's most vicious right wing death squads, the Argentine Anti-Communist Alliance, and was forced to emigrate to Mexico, where she has lived and worked ever since. In the past 14 years, Langer has helped to organize movements which denounce the violations of human rights in countries such as Argentina, Chile, El Salvador and Guatemala, and has treated victims of torture and other human rights abuses, many of whom are women. Since 1981, she has been the Co-coordinator of the Internationalist Team of Mental Health Workers, a group of 12 Latin American psychoanalysts, psychiatrists and psychologists residing in Mexico who travel monthly on a rotating basis to Nicaragua, where they are assisting the Sandinista government in the development of a national mental health system. Langer is profoundly enthusiastic about this work and grateful for the opportunity to contribute her energy and skills to a country in which a commitment to radical social transformation exists alongside an interest in a psychoanalytically-informed understanding of human psychology.

With this introduction to Langer's life, we shall now turn to an exploration of the ways in which she has integrated Marxism, feminism and psychoanalysis in her theoretical work, clinical practice and political activism with women.

MELANIE KLEIN AND FEMALE SEXUALITY

In 1942, Langer was the only woman among the six founding members of the Argentine Psychoanalytic Association, which was recognized by the International Psychoanalytic Association the following year. By the early 1950s, psychoanalysis would become

highly fashionable among the European-identified cosmopolitan
middle class of Buenos Aires, penetrating both the academy and
popular culture. The Argentine Psychoanalytic Association would
also become the center of psychoanalytic training for all of Latin
America for a period, especially Brazil, Mexico and Uruguay. In
the formative years, there were only a few practicing female ana-
lysts, and colleagues tended to refer female patients to Langer,
some of whom suffered from problems associated with sterility and
infertility. While Langer's treatment did not focus on these particular symptoms, a notable impact of therapy was the apparent resolu-
tion of fundamental conflicts associated with motherhood, resulting
in successful pregnancies. This experience led Langer to become
interested in developing a specialty in psychosomatic illnesses associated with reproduction. In her search for a theoretical framework
within psychoanalysis which could adequately address this conflictual female state, she was led to reject Freud's ideas about female
sexuality because of their phallocentric assumptions, which she
found incomprehensible and not applicable clinically (Langer,
1981, p. 153). In the early 1940s, Langer studied Melanie Klein
and supervised the translation of her work into Spanish. While critical of Klein's theory of female development for its failure to link
female mental states to social conditions and cultural values, she
nonetheless found in Klein's approach to female sexual development an acceptance of woman's innate reproductive capacity and an
exploration of a specifically female psychobiological experience,
including unconscious phantasies and anxieties that exist from infancy on, related directly to this latent reproductive ability.

It is important here to summarize Klein's fundamental concepts
which Langer integrated into her conceptualization of the psychogenesis of psychosomatic disturbances in female sexual and reproductive life. According to Langer, Klein correctly understood that
the oedipal complex begins in the first year of life, rather than the
fourth year as Freud had maintained. Klein asserted that the infant
reacts to the frustrations that she suffers at the maternal breast,
which in the first months of life represents the mother herself or at
least her most important part. The infant imagines that the father
has a similar organ, but better and more generous, which is later
identified with the father's penis. The female also experiences a

disillusionment with her mother, who she imagines prefers her father, whom she feeds more generously than herself. The girl thus enters into a state of rivalry with her father and feels resentment toward her mother. Envy toward the mother is reinforced because the girl also imagines that the father feeds the mother with his penis, filling her with penises, children and milk. This early hatred toward the mother motivates the girl to wish to destroy the interior of the maternal body and to appropriate the desired objects for herself. Consequently, the girl fears her mother's retaliation against her own body, and the subsequent destruction of her female organs. Klein believed that the anxieties experienced by the girl occur earlier in her development than concomitant fears experienced by the boy, because she cannot yet know about the integrity of her genitals and because motherhood is only a potential achievement in the far future.

Klein postulated that penis envy is a secondary and defensive phenomenon, a neurotic posture emerging from the girl's early oedipal complex unleashed by oral frustrations with the mother. The girl adopts from the beginning a feminine and passive attitude toward the father, and, aware of her vagina, wishes to have the paternal penis inside her. But in the frustration of her oedipal desires, the girl directs sadistic phantasies toward the penis, and, having projected her own aggression onto this organ, ends up fearing its contact. Frustrated by the father and envious of him, she develops an identification with him. This defensive posture involves the unconscious belief that she has introjected her father's penis and, now in possession of it, can receive all she desires from her mother.

For Langer, Klein's challenge of Freud's idea that the infant relates ambivalently to the maternal breast and the paternal penis was important. According to Klein, the infant has the representation of a good breast, which gives milk, and a bad breast, which frustrates its needs. Thus the infant splits its objects into good and bad. Confusing phantasy with reality, the infant believes it has introjected a quantity of bad objects and anxiously searches for good objects in the external world to incorporate and neutralize the destructive action of the bad objects. It also attempts to project the bad objects

carried inside. Klein indicated that the infant's unconscious phantasy world is mitigated to a great extent by the real parental response to its projections and introjections. The severity of the unconscious drama is gradually reduced if in reality there is a good
and nurturing mother (and father) and the strength of the internal
good objects can come to mirror the good objects in the environment. Thus through love of her child, the real mother can help to
minimize the effects of the internal conflictual world that typifies
the early mental states of the human infant.

Langer believed that Klein's depiction of the unconscious phantasy life of the infant was extraordinarily theoretical and often difficult to grasp or accept. However, it helped her to interpret very
concrete problems that emerged in her clinical practice over an
eight year period, most of which was with Argentine middle class
women. While her female patients often manifested penis envy,
castration feelings and a masculine identification, she came to understand these phenomena as defenses against more profound conflicts related to the fears of destruction of one's femininity. For
example, in reaction to the onset of menstruation, many of Langer's
patients manifested a contradictory mixture of humiliation, disgust
and joy. Langer interpreted the humiliation and disgust as corres-
ponding to the loss of a supposed virility, a kind of castration, while
the joy was the consequence of the relief experienced of an intact
femininity in which the irrational fears of having been destroyed
internally by a vindictive mother were dispelled. In its positive association, menstruation signified the promise of future motherhood
and the realization of a specifically female psychobiological potential.

THE PSYCHOSOCIAL CONTRADICTIONS
OF MOTHERHOOD

In 1951, Langer published *Motherhood and Sexuality*, a book
that was to bring her notoriety throughout Latin America for its
groundbreaking study of the psychogenesis of frequently encoun-
tered problems in female reproductive functions. The book contains
chapters on menstruation, pregnancy, breastfeeding, sterility and
infertility, and menopause. Langer's work set her apart from her

North American and European counterparts in psychoanalysis who were publishing books in the fifties asserting that female psychological conflicts would only be resolved through an acceptance of the "feminine" role of wife and mother in the domestic sphere and an abandonment of competitive ambitions in the public world of men. From Langer's perspective, woman's conflictual relationship to sexuality and motherhood would only be resolved through the successful challenge to the legal, social and economic institutions which confined her to the home and limited her creative endeavors in the public sphere. Langer's study predated the current feminist movement by several decades in its attempt to contextualize the specific psychological issues she discussed within a Marxist historical analysis of the origins of patriarchal culture and the subordinate status of women. This account of patriarchy was the starting point, from Langer's perspective, for any legitimate discussion of female intrapsychic problems. Utilizing Margaret Meade's anthropological studies, she also aimed at a comparative approach to indicate the cultural specificity of the female psychological problems she examined based on her own clinical cases.

Langer offered the following thesis as the context for her study. Until the twentieth century, society had imposed severe sexual and social restrictions on women, favoring the development of their maternal functions. The consequences of these restrictions and the repression of female creative energy very frequently included hysteria and other neurotic symptoms. Women seldom seemed to suffer from psychosomatic difficulties in their reproductive functions. Langer then pointed to the change since the turn of the century in this situation for women in Western culture. Women have acquired sexual and social liberties hardly imagined in earlier times, with attendant restrictions imposed on the mothering role by cultural and economic circumstances. Hysteria as the general neurotic picture had been replaced by a dramatic increase in psychosomatic problems of sterility and infertility, which occured among women who did not necessarily manifest a general picture of neurosis. The clinical cases Langer discussed in this book reveal patients who suffered from a basic conflict regarding their femininity.

The book contains an awesome amount of clinical case material, which for lack of space, cannot be reproduced here. Rather than

describe individual cases that reveal Langer's analytic interpretations, we will select one aspect of her study, summarizing her discussion of the impact that unconscious conflict and anxieties have
on pregnancy and childbirth (Langer, 1951, Chapter 10).

Arguing that the maternal instinct is an integral part of female
sexuality, Langer asserted that when realized, it gratifies multiple
desires of woman. A woman wants a child because it signifies the
recuperation of her own mother and permits an identification with
her. She also desires a child in order to confirm her own fertility.
The wish for a child may correspond to an infantile desire to give a
child to her father or may represent the unconsciously desired penis.
The rational and conscious factors that influence the hope for a
child include the desire to relive her own infancy through it or to
give to it that which she herself never had (reparation). She may be
motivated by rivalry with other women, pressure to keep her husband or acquisition of status as defined by patriarchal expectations
of woman's roles. But fundamentally, a woman's desire to bear a
child stems from a psychobiological need to develop all of her latent
capacities.

Various psychoanalytic theories had shown that women repeat
during pregnancy and birth their own infantile experience, especially their primitive relationship to their own mothers, including
the ambivalence which characterizes it. However, Langer observed
that the fetus could acquire other meanings, most frequently that it
is experienced unconsciously as something stolen from the mother.
Thus the adult pregnant woman may relive much of the infantile
unconscious phantasy of having robbed her mother of the valuable
contents of her body, with the concomitant fear of mother's retaliation. In such cases, many kinds of somatic difficulties may arise.
One of the possible reactions is the unconscious rejection of the
fetus: if the pregnant woman identifies with the fetus, she projects
onto it her own infantile greed and her earliest phantasies of con-
suming her mother. When the fetus represents her mother, whose
oral retribution the woman fears, it is experienced as something
destructive that she carries within her. According to Langer, those
women who fear they will give birth to some kind of monstrously

deformed creature reveal in this fear a judgment that their own infantile desires were monstrous and that in the demands they made on their mothers, they behaved as monsters. This fear of giving birth to a monster stems as well from the fear of one's own destructive sentiments toward the child, who may represent either the husband, father or brother—something that unconsciously belongs to the mother.

While the woman suffering from sterility may unconsciously interpret her inability to become pregnant as a punishment imposed by her mother, the pregnant woman may experience the fetus as a dangerous trap set by her mother, and the pregnancy itself becomes a punishment. The woman with these unconscious associations may react with semiconscious intents to miscarry, and subsequently suffer from profound guilt feelings. A difficult pregnancy, with exaggerated physical symptoms of discomfort is often an indication of the conflicts described above. The most common psychosomatic difficulties are of an oral and anal type. Nausea, vomiting and eating binges, for example, may represent an unconscious and irrational attempt to orally abort the fetus and the defense against this wish. In diarrhea and constipation, the wish to abort and the defense against it are lived out in a regression to the anal phase and can be more of a danger to the continuation of the pregnancy. In miscarriage, the unconscious hostile tendencies toward the pregnancy are so strong that they are victorious.

Langer argued that psychosomatic illness associated with pregnancy may be resolved when the unconscious conflict underlying the problem is addressed. In her experience, psychoanalytic treatment which was able to achieve an identification on the part of the patient with her mother facilitated in Kleinian terms the reparation with the internal maternal object, resulting in the ability of the patient to actualize the wish to have a baby.

With respect to childbirth itself, Langer observed that in spite of all the scientific advances reducing the actual danger and pain associated with delivery, women still approach the experience with fear and anxiety. This is because the birth itself has unconscious significance in which all the irrational fears that were especially vivid during the beginning of the pregnancy are revived. Only now with the appearance of her infant will a woman truly know the nature of what she has carried inside her and created; only at that moment will she know if her insides are intact, if her mother has not punished her, and if she, through her badness, has not damaged her child. Equally important, the positive feelings usually typical of the last part of a pregnancy now function as a source of anxiety of another sort. In this case, the birth is the revival of the oldest and most archaic anguish we know, that of the separation from the mother. The woman, identified with her child, lives through childbirth all of the fears of separating from her mother. She identifies with the abandonment of the child and feels that she cannot continue to protect it against the vicissitudes of life. She feels that the infant loses its mother and simultaneously experiences the birth as a loss of the child. Langer warned that without recourse to modern methods of childbirth, which facilitate the pregnant woman's waking and aware participation in the childbirth itself and an immediate bonding with the baby, these anxieties would continue to characterize the experience of giving birth.

Langer reiterated throughout her study that these vicissitudes of motherhood and sexuality are found among women for whom their relationship with their mothers had been frustrating, mutually resentful and destructive. She reminded her readers that the infant's dramatic unconscious phantasy life could be rendered more or less benign through a positive environment, i.e., a loving parental involvement. However, careful not to blame women for the objective conditions that might impede their fulfillment of this important function for their children, Langer looked to historical and sociological reasons for "maternal failure" to provide a good-enough environment capable of producing relatively conflict-free daughters who embrace their specifically female psychosexual potential.

Referring to the traditional gendered division of labor, Langer argued that the classic belief in the natural inferiority of women had many functions and was sustained by social and psychological factors. The latter stem from earliest infancy, in which the child resents the mother for its complete dependency on her and for her inability in phantasy or reality to satisfy its every need. This fear of dependency is complicated by the infant's unconscious rivalry, envy and fear. These early sentiments remain as an unconscious fear of the omnipotent mother, which is expressed defensively within patriarchy through the social control of women. This psychological basis for maintaining women in a status of inferiority was rationalized through an ideological apparatus which induced an attitude of resignation among women toward the limited parameters of their lives. Deprived of socially acceptable avenues of discharge, women expressed their conflict within the family constellation. Until well into the twentieth century this division of labor, though detrimental to women, maintained social stability and provided both male and female with a set of strictly defined and predictable expectations.

In the contemporary period, increasing opportunities for women had resulted in confusion regarding expectations about women's role. For middle class married women, the norms of conduct were no longer well defined. The combination of maternal and professional aspirations represented complex new pressures. The female was now expected to bear and raise children, keep a job with hours and duties like her husband, be responsible for the housework and maintain herself physically attractive and psychologically available for her husband. These multiple roles, presented as new possibilities for self-realization, in reality resulted in increasing demands with a built-in guarantee of failure. Any woman in this situation was destined to feel inadequate to the task in every arena. Self-blame was usually her reaction. On the other hand, the middle class married woman who decided to dedicate herself mainly to her children and husband found that her work was increasingly devalued because of its invisibility and that she felt less empowered than her husband and professional women because she was not earning money for her work. Langer was convinced that this relatively new situation for women caused increased conflictual attitudes toward their children, a pattern that was damaging in very specific ways for women of the following generation. Women who were trapped in situations that engendered feelings of self-hate and anguish about their lives as women could not help but transmit these conflicts to their daughters, who in turn bore the burden of an unconscious

identification with these attitudes and feelings. This situation, embedded as it was in the gendered arrangements of patriarchy, could
only be altered if the social, economic and ideological institutions
changed in order to support the right of a woman to work in a
satisfying manner outside the home and to enjoy the fulfillment of
being a mother. Part of Langer's feminist vision of change included
the necessity of the early participation of the father in the life of
children, which would allow infants and youngsters to develop deep
affective ties to both parents, thus escaping the total dependence on
mother which engenders so much fear and resentment. The active
involvement of the father from the birth of the infant would also
allow for the acquisition of gender identity which would not be
associated with an exaggerated differentiation of social roles and
psychological traits attributed to males and females.

Langer focused on the dilemma of middle class women, mainly
because they were the source of her clinical work from which she
drew much of her material. She was aware that the psychological
crisis for working class women was framed by their situation within
the class/gender system, and she would have the opportunity to
work directly with this sector of the female population years later as
part of her political commitment to democratize the mental health
professions and facilitate access to psychoanalytically informed
psychotherapy to patients in public hospital settings. Her insights
stemming from this important experience will be described below.

Motherhood and Sexuality first appeared in 1951, and while
some of its Marxist and feminist perspectives are now very familiar
ones, they were remarkably provocative for their time. The subject
of psychogenic problems in female reproduction has rarely been
conceptualized in quite the same manner as Langer has offered us.
In fact, her study may be even more salient today than it was almost
40 years ago, given the apparently increasing numbers of women
who suffer from infertility in the contemporary period. Perhaps this
explains the fact that in the last five years new editions of Langer's
book have been published in Latin America, Spain, Portugal, West
Germany and Italy.

Langer's Kleinian object relations approach offers a stimulating
view that differs from most contemporary feminist psychoanalytic

studies. In the Lacanian tradition, there is an emphasis on an analysis of the unconscious acquisition of gender characteristics through the oedipal stage that makes a good "fit" with the sexual division of labor in capitalist society. This perspective stresses the "deficits" of women's socialization. Other recent works suggest a positive evaluation of women's psychology resulting from socialization in patriarchal culture. It is argued that due to their nurturing relationship with infants and young children, women have the capacity to tolerate exposure to unconscious processes in daily life, a mode that stands in stark contrast to the demands of the routinized and rational order of the public sphere of capitalist society that deprive men of valued attributes. Langer's analysis shares many of the conclusions of these studies, but addresses different issues as well. She attempts to account for the intensely conflictual internal world that she believes characterizes both males and females in culturally determined unique ways. Her feminist view of women does not depict them as internally harmonious, but rather capable of sadistic and rage-filled sentiments and actions. While she views the mother/ child relationship as the central mediating factor in human psychological development, she does not romanticize it. And although her perspective emphasizes greed, envy and hate as elementary human emotions, it also offers a view of human psychology that contains the potential for intimate connectedness. Langer's view asserts that infantile forces of rage and hate are capable of being integrated and resolved if others are available to help the infant share the burden of its pain and anxiety. There is an emphasis here on the primacy of social relations in the normal maturational process. And significantly, there is a great stress placed on the possibilities of profound positive emotions of love and genuine concern for others. In Klein's concept of reparation, artistic endeavors are understood to be related to the recovery and restoration of damaged and lost internal objects. Such activity thus becomes a symbolic preservation of the relationship to a loved object. For Langer, political ideals and movements which aim to create a social order based on cooperation rather than exploitation may be understood in the same way, and the elimination of the class/gender system becomes a theoretical possibility because of this human impulse toward reparation (Rustin, 1982).

MARXIST FEMINIST POLITICS
AND PSYCHOANALYSIS

From her perspective, Langer has had the good fortune to live in the Third World, where undeniable conditions of class exploitation and political repression have combined to facilitate an active engagement by Marxists and psychoanalysts in the struggle toward a just and equitable social order. From the late 1960s on, Langer assumed a leadership role in the movement of radical dissident psychoanalysts who left the Argentine Psychoanalytic Association because of its elitist internal structure and its affiliation with the dominant class of Argentine society. As political conditions in general polarized, Langer and her progressive colleagues aligned themselves with workers, unemployed, students and middle class professionals and entrepreneurs who fought against a series of dictatorships determined to shore up a system in crisis. Profits for United States-based multinationals and the Argentine capitalist class were gained at the cost of rising unemployment, escalating inflation, declining services in health and welfare and marked excesses in political repression. The activities of these politically committed mental health professionals took many forms, the details of which are beyond the scope of this article (Hollander, 1984). We shall focus here on describing two examples of Langer's contributions, the first one a clinical experience and the second one a theoretical publication, that relate directly to her feminist convictions.

As part of the effort to democratize the psychoanalytic profession and make the training and skills of this traditionally elite practice available to the working class, Langer and several colleagues initiated a research project which involved group therapy in a public hospital where many working class housewives were requesting treatment for depression (Langer et al., 1972). It was observed that the majority of these women were characterized by immature personality development and reactive depressions, while the rest of them suffered from less specifically defined conditions, including vague anxiety feelings, weepiness, exhaustion, and the lack of mature affective capacity and sexual responsiveness. Half of the women manifested various forms of hypochondria. Most had developed these symptoms upon marrying and becoming housewives and mothers, and they remembered with nostalgia the days when they had worked outside the home. Now their entire social existence and affective ties were related exclusively to their families. Usually years of a pervasive sensation of boredom had given way to acute depression precipitated by the loss of a parent or a rift with a mother or one of the children. These women all maintained a dependent relationship with their mothers and lived in fear of being judged by them.

This project was different from others in Argentina that had examined the neurotic effects of the lifestyle of the housewife; it explored the sexual life of its subjects as well as the ideology marking their conscious life. The purpose of the study was to analyze the living conditions and psychopathology of the women of Argentina's working class and to examine the pathogenic conditions of the conflictual family structure. Langer and her colleagues noted the following contradictions characteristic of the existing situation: within the traditional extended family, an almost total submissiveness was required of women, reinforced by expectations expressed through a complex network of social relations; within the nuclear family, women found themselves isolated and without affective connections. In a desperate attempt to conserve some intimate contact, many clung to their mothers, which not only resolved nothing, but complicated their psychosocial development, making a healthy individuation impossible. Over time, their husbands became disinterested in their wives sexually and emotionally. They refused to allow their wives to work outside the home, and rarely included them in a shared circle of mutual friends.

However, contrary to the bourgeois feminist demands of equal access to work, these wives of working class men did not see in the labor market a way out of their dilemma. For them, not working in a factory, at least in the short run, had meant the elimination of the "double day." These working class women had opted for domesticity, which, although suffocating, was less exploitative than the work imposed by their employers. Ironically, the apparent liberation of the housewife role engendered the psychopathology analyzed in the study.

In the group psychotherapy with these patients, Langer and her colleagues, all of whom had a political critique of the class and gender system which they viewed as responsible for the psychopathology apparent in their female patients, had to decide on an appropriate model of intervention and whether direct suggestions regarding return to work or participation in political and union struggles was justified as part of a therapeutic intervention. What follows is one example of the way in which Langer resolved the question of how a politically engaged psychoanalyst could retain a technique based fundamentally on interpretation.

Langer co-authored a paper in which she critiqued the idea of therapeutic neutrality. She asserted that every intervention on the part of a therapist carries with it an ideological perspective, conscious or unconscious, making neutrality in the therapeutic posture an impossibility (Langer, 1973, 1985). She offered the following episode in one group therapy session as an example of her contention. In this group, Langer was the principal therapist and supervised two additional female psychologists who were her co-therapists. One patient, pregnant with her first child, spoke about wanting to pursue a college education in order to avoid a future that duplicated the frustrating life of her mother. In response, one of the psychologists interpreted: "You want to surpass your mother." This was apparently a "correct" intervention and nothing more. But, suggested Langer, if one examined the latent message, it was an ideological and culturally prejudiced intervention, because it implied that to desire to surpass one's mother is bad. Why? Because the culture, and that which we have internalized in the superego, carries injunctions against surpassing one's parents, a prohibition which ensures that the family and class relations will remain the same. The other psychologist then intervened: "You are competitive with your husband." The patient's husband also worked and was a student, and the patient would have to abandon both her job and her studies once the baby was born. One of the other patients commented that at least the woman had her pregnancy, and another patient rejoined by asserting that the patient's husband, like her father too, had a penis. Langer commented that this biological difference is a reality, but perhaps it should not mean that one doesn't struggle to change destiny. The question is, how? Individually? Knowing that the patient's husband was also active in leftist politics, Langer intervened in the following manner: "It is true that you would like to go beyond your mother's possibilities and have the same opportunity as your husband. And why not? It is your right. But there are two avenues to achieve this; struggle oneself for an individual solution or struggle collectively so that everyone can change these conditions of deprivation."

Langer analyzed the significance of the three interventions. She suggested that the first ("you are competing with your mother") was strictly an oedipal interpretation, one directed at the child within the adult woman who continues to compete for her father. The second interpretation ("you are competing with your husband") pointed to penis envy; that is, the negative oedipal complex, and its implicit goal was to help the patient work through this envy, discard it and adopt a "feminine" attitude toward the husband-father, accepting the child as a substitute for the penis. For this patient, it would mean renouncing first her studies and then, over time with the acquisition of a degree of economic security, her paid work. For Langer, these two oedipal interpretations tended to transform a "rebellious" woman into a submissive housewife and future patient. Dedicated to the invisible labor in the home, this woman would live as her mother had, in total emotional dependency on her husband-father and on her child, the only visible product of her labor. She will be more infantile than her husband, with less capacity to sublimate. Her own low self-esteem would provoke envy of her husband's involvements, including even political activity. Thus, these two interventions, though made in good faith at the conscious level with little intention of supporting the existing patriarchal family, represented at the unconscious level an ideology supportive of the existing class/gender system.

Langer then addressed the significance of her own intervention:

the first part ("It is true that you would like to go beyond your
mother and have the same opportunities as your husband. And why
not? It is your right") dealt with the oedipal material, but it tried to
suggest that the patient discriminate between her infantile desires
and her rights as an adult woman. The second part ("But there are
two avenues to achieve this; struggle oneself for an individual solution or struggle collectively . . .") pointed to another aspect of the
oedipal drama and of human history. It alluded not to the husband-
father, but to the husband-brother. Here Langer summarized
Freud's famous study, *Totem and Taboo*, in which Freud described
the origins of the oedipal complex. Freud argued that at the down of
human history the horde of brothers allied themselves in the murder
of the tyrannical father who had exploited them and who, in order to
possess all of the women, had expelled his sons when they reached
sexual maturity. After the father's murder, the sons consumed his
remains, thus introjecting the power of the father as a superego.
Then, obeying the superego injunction, incest with mothers and
sisters of the horde was forbidden, so that the crime would not be
repeated. When we speak of the oedipal complex, asserted Langer,
we almost always refer to the prohibition against the desire of the
son for the mother and his competition with the father. In doing so,
she claimed, we ignore another important situation, equally prohibited and repressed by the superego, that is prior to the oedipal
crime: the alliance among the brothers. We can deduce, she argued,
that the most "criminal" and thus the most prohibited and repressed by the paternal superego is the conquest of the mutual jeal-
ousy among brothers in order to dethrone the father. Interpreted in
terms of social organization, we are speaking of putting solidarity
among comrades ahead of individual and family welfare and respect
for the established authority. So, Langer concluded, to speak to the
patient of the "second alternative" indicates to her implicitly that
she should not confuse her husband with her father, but symboli-
cally see him as equivalent to her brother. Then she would ally
herself with him and other comrades against the system, as she
could have done in her infancy against her parents, only now as an
adult and with a common political goal.

This critical approach in her clinical work was mirrored in
Langer's writings of the same period. As part of her active role in

the dissident movement within established psychoanalysis, she was one of the editors of two important collections of articles published in 1971 and 1973, entitled *Cuestionamos I* and *Cuestionamos II* [We Question], in which many aspects of the relationship between psychoanalysis and social change were analyzed. In the first volume, Langer's contribution was her controversial paper delivered at the International Psychoanalytic Association Convention in Vienna in July 1971, titled "Psychoanalysis and/or Social Revolution." In this paper, which traced the points of conjunction between Marx and Freud, she asserted the inevitability of radical transformation of contemporary society and urged her colleagues to use their psychoanalytic knowledge to facilitate rather than oppose the process of change. In the second volume, Langer's contribution, "Woman: Her Limits and Potential," was an explicit attempt to demonstrate the convergence of aspects of Marxism, psychoanalysis and feminism in an assessment of the specific nature of women's oppression. She agreed with the contemporary Marxist feminist analysis of women's labor in capitalist society, which is characterized by the elaboration of use value for direct and private consumption within the family. Woman is segregated from the world of surplus value where the products of labor are economically visible and destined to create wealth through exchange value in the market. Woman's labor, essential to the system through its maintenance and reproduction of labor power, is invisible because it receives no monetary remuneration or status. The nature of domestic work is its repetitive quality, the only visible product the woman produces being her child. Langer went on to demonstrate from a psychoanalytic perspective the ways in which this social arrangement and the demands to adapt to it are internalized as part of the superego, so that women remain divested of a critical conscious awareness of the structural source of their sense of inferiority and conflictual relationship to their work and intimate relations.

In this article, Langer suggested that the family is the central ideological mediating institution of the class/gender system, and should be critically reevaluated in terms of its destructive impact on women. Sharing with radical feminists their view that women should control their own bodies in sexual pleasure and reproduction, Langer critiqued as ideology and not science the traditional assumptions within psychoanalysis which condemned women to define themselves passively in terms of their relationship to men and children. And she asserted that the feminist visions of replacing the male-dominated/female-centered nuclear family with social arrangements emphasizing cooperation and sharing rather than possession between the sexes and the generations could become a reality only with the elimination of the class system.

What is the role of feminist movements in this struggle? Langer argues that an independent feminist movement mobilized to challenge capitalist class relations and patriarchal culture is a necessary part of revolutionary struggle. She is critical of feminist ideology and politics which she considers to be essentially anti-male, and warns against confusing the battle against patriarchy with a battle against men. From her psychoanalytic perspective, women's hostility against men is a symptom, that is, a compromise formation between repressed thoughts or feelings and the defense against them. She believes that the anguish and hostility that is provoked in the struggle for emancipation originates in the early relationship with the mother and is displaced secondarily onto the male. The elaboration of the original conflictual relationship is necessary to free women's political energies. Women who seek a connection only with other women regress to a preoedipal relationship via the wish to become merged with the generous and omnipotent mother. In this desire, argues Langer, women deny their own hostility as well as the other image of the mother—the omnipotent and frightening one. This image is displaced onto the male and thus preserves the good internal mother. The possibility of autonomy and emancipation, of achieving maturity, including motherhood, has been abandoned. Having said this, Langer reaffirms the absolute necessity of a strong and independent feminist movement: feminism without Marxism, she asserts, cannot achieve structural change, but Marxist parties are not sufficient to carry out the struggle for the rights and needs of women. "One has to be a woman, to have experienced in one's own guts our insecurity, our doubts, our overwork and marginalization, in order to recognize all that has to change" (*Memoria*, 228). Langer believes that a strong autonomous women's movement must act as a pressure from the outside to push Marxist parties in the implementation of their self-declared commitment to fight for changes in the social, political and economic conditions that oppress women.

Langer recently commented that she had finally, in her seventies, discovered the common denominator of Marxism, psychoanalysis and feminism, the three fundamental interests of her life. That common denominator is consciousness: the consciousness to be able to achieve change (*Memoria* 231).

From the mid-1970s on, Langer has been clear about how she can best use her psychoanalytic skills, feminist convictions and political commitment in the service of change. She has treated many victims of state terror from various countries in Latin America who suffer from post-traumatic stress disorder, often helping female patients to deal with the impact that horrendously abusive experiences have had on their self-esteem and their relationships to mates and children. In her role as the Co-coordinator of the Internationalist Team of Mental Health Workers, who are contributing to the creation of a national mental health system in Nicaragua, Langer has participated in establishing training programs and clinical services, many of which focus on the special psychological needs of women and children.

Marie Langer, 77 years old, continues to live according to deeply held principles which she believes are expressed in her work in Nicaragua:

> I don't want to die for free, to die without meaning—I want to live until the end. So when the dangers of the Nicaraguan work emerge, I always remember an article by Mao that I read once in which he speaks of the death that is worth something and one that has no value. He was speaking of the individual who has some worth in life, some weight in history. How terrible is the useless life, the useless death. I believe this very much, and I believe that my life has been worthy, within my own limits. I don't want to die gratuitously . . . so that's why the work in Nicaragua is important for what I believe my life signifies. (Langer, 1986)

REFERENCES

Hollander, N. (1985). Marie Langer: Psychoanalysis in the service of the people. *Psych Critique*, I(1).

Langer, M. (1951). *Materndid y sexo*, Buenos Aires.

Langer, M. (1981). *Memoria, historia y dialogo psicoanalitico*, Buenos Aires.

Langer, M., et al. (1971 and 1973). *Cuestionamos I and II*, Buenos Aires.

Langer, M. (1985). Interview with Hollander, N.

Langer, M. (1986). Interview with Hollander, N.

Rustin, M. (1982). A socialist consideration of Kleinian psychoanalysis. *New Left Review*, 131.

Visit to the Dentist: Dialectics

"Your teeth reflect your psychic life,"
says he.
"My teeth reflect my poverty,"
say I.

My father doesn't have a tooth in his head.
My mother has one.
My brother's teeth were pulled
when he was sixteen;
The Army gave him dentures
when he was seventeen and joined.
My sister had false teeth at twenty-four.
I've had twenty-three teeth (I counted them)
since I was thirty.
Progress no doubt.
At thirteen I came to the land of opportunity
I also had my first two teeth pulled.

My psychic life reflects my poverty.
The X rays of my teeth
are the pictures of my life.
There they are:
Front teeth standing straight
(more or less)
Back teeth crouching
(And some reclining)
begging to be forgotten.
Transparent teeth
with opaque patches

Martha Chabrán is a writer, presently working on a novel and autobiography. She taught Spanish at the Regional College of Inter-American University in Guayana, Puerto Rico.

"Visit to the Dentist: Dialectics" appeared in *Heresies*. It is reprinted here with permission of the authors and *Heresies*.

where the wounds were plastered
to protect the nerve
from heat and cold and pain.

From heat and cold and pain.

Martha Chabrán

Poor Women of Color
Do Great Therapy

Lenora Fulani

In 1987, the Harlem Institute for Social Therapy and Research, located on 125th Street and Seventh Avenue in the landmark Theresa Hotel, serves, in my opinion, as a model of how to build among the Black, Latino, Jewish, lesbian and gay, and other oppressed populations of this country a deeply needed, deeply missed, inclusive, and empowering *sense of community* based on the power *of* and love *for* the oppressed.

This sense of community is not new to my ancestors. African-American historians teach us of African communalism, the collective practice and spirit that dominated the work and lifestyles of our people before the European raping of the African continent, a spirit that remains profoundly visible in the liberation struggles of contemporary Namibia, Zimbabwe, Angola, Mozambique, the Congo, and South Africa as ancient African communalism is shaped into a critical tool in their respective fights for freedom and justice. It is a spirit and a vision that appeared time and time again in the leadership of Dr. King, Malcolm X, and the Black Panthers. And it is raising its proud head today in the leadership women of color pro-

Lenora Fulani, PhD, is an internationally known political leader and developmental psychologist. Currently, she is Director of the Community Clinics at the Institute for Social Therapy and Research. In 1988, Dr. Fulani is an independent candidate for President of the U.S. Dr. Fulani is Chair of the Women of Color Caucus of the New Alliance Party, and ran for governor of New York State in 1986 as the only Black, the only woman, and the only progressive candidate. She is in demand as a speaker for federal, state and local organizations with expertise on issues such as Black psychology, multi-racialism, and the gay community. Dr. Fulani's pioneering work at her Harlem clinic serves as a model for inner-city community empowerment.

vide to the Blacks, Latinos, Jews, lesbians and gay men, and pro-
gressives in the community of which the Institute for Social Therapy and Research (ISTR) is a part. Racist and sexist America has
always attempted to deprive its people of a sense of community.
The powers that be use whatever means they deem necessary to
undermine this sense of community and its accompaniment, a sense
of history. Black folks are stereotypically denigrated by the ideological lackeys of those who rule as a people who don't stick together: Blacks and Latinos and Asians as people who can't unite
because we come from radically different cultures; Blacks and gays
as almost genetically incompatible; Jews as people who do stick
together, but only for themselves, etc. Those in control have spent
billions of dollars and trillions of conniving hours destroying
grassroots movements, leaders, and peoples. For they are aware
that the development of a real sense of community, of history, and
of solidarity is a profound threat to their exploitative system of rule.

Under these circumstances, how do we build community in our
day-to-day practice at the Institute for Social Therapy and Research? It is from the vantage point of this inquiry that we best study
Social Therapy, a drug-free, group-oriented approach to the treatment of emotional problems that is deeply steeped in a recognition
that our problems — so-called mental illness and the more ordinary
emotional stresses of our daily lives — are social in both their origins
and their character.

IN THE BEGINNING

I remember when I first began practicing at the Harlem Institute
(one of the five locations in the New York City area of our Community Clinics) how taken aback I was that poor people and addicted
people in our Medicaid groups would walk in with descriptions and
"understandings" of themselves and their problems that were
straight out of Ronald Reagan's mouth; that the Black and Latino
professional middle class would come in with identities from Ozzie
and Harriet and the Cosby's and would ask, "Why me?" as if they
were not also Black and Latino; and that gay people would display
no sense that being gay in America is a radical posture that seriously

challenges some basic and oppressive institutions of this society, e.g., the traditional family.

But in a relatively short time within the heterogeneous Social Therapy groups, Black and Latino sisters and brothers—middle class, working class, and poor—opened up secrets that they had kept for years, secrets of incest, affairs, gay relationships, drug and alcohol addiction, "dirty" thoughts, possessions, obsessions, self-hatred, self-doubt, inadequacies, humiliations, and failures. I heard adults who grew up as foster children and who were taught that anything they got was more than they deserved say, "I, too, can have something"; menacingly macho men talk about homosexual relationships in their adolescence, and for the first time raise their heads as they recognized that those relationships were the most intimate they had ever had with anyone and not something to be ashamed of; Caribbean Americans weep openly for the first time of their mistreatment at the hands of Black Americans; Puerto Rican women and men—in English and Spanish—make demands and stop being invisible. I saw the chronically ill improve their health for the first time in decades from getting the proper dosages of compassion and ruthlessness, *not* drugs; poor Jews in the Bronx fight back against the vicious anti-Semitism that says you can't be Jewish and poor in contemporary America; gay people come out; straight people loosen up; women be powerful; men struggle to be intimate; and poor people kick ass! I saw our peoples—different peoples—our community, becoming empowered. Women of color played the key role in this seemingly amazing process. Why and how?

THE CONTRADICTION

Women of color have a profoundly conflicted relationship to the institution of therapy. More than most people, to us being in therapy means that we have failed in our roles as (super) women. Women of color who come to us for therapy see themselves not as having problems, but *as the problem*. If a woman of color cannot succeed as a mother, a wife, a grandmother, even (actually especially) under the worst of conditions, then there is something wrong with *her*. She has failed. *She is the problem*.

In fact, the woman of color—while not the *problem*—is a contradiction within this society. What is that contradiction? To put the
matter all too simply, it looks something like this. The primary or
paradigmatic role for women of color is to socialize other people of
color to adapt to a society that is structurally racist, sexist, classist
and homophobic—a society whose standard for what is normal is
white, male, middle class and heterosexual. Thus the *societal function* of women of color is to help others adapt to a situation which is
fundamentally alien to them, i.e., to do the impossible. Indeed, this
is a task for a superwoman. Societally speaking, women of color
are set up to fail. For while some people of color—most often, men
of color—"make it" into the white society many, many do not.
Moreover, assimilation typically means denying our cultural/histor-
ical identity to varying degrees. Hence, raising a child who "makes
it" implies another adult who has been "shaped by the institutions
of her or his oppressor." Even when by societal standards the
woman of color succeeds, by virtue of her success, she is further
estranged from her child, who is now vastly more assimilated than
she is and with a personality utterly foreign to her or his "socializ-
ing-woman-of-color." The woman of color *syndrome* characteristi-
cally means failure—or failure.

But women of color (like everyone else) have a historical/cultural
function as well as a societal one. And the historical role of the
woman of color is diametrically opposed to her societal role. In
history, the woman of color's role is to support the identity of her
family members as people of color within the context of the historical struggle of oppressed peoples for liberation. These women of
color function to adapt people of color to our culture and history,
not to the alien society in which we reside. In the performance of
this historical activity, the woman of color recognizes the critical
importance of community. Thus, the woman of color is not only in
a contradictory position within her societal role, but as well her
societal role is in contradiction to her historical/cultural role.

This distinction between societal role and historical role (society
and history) is crucial to understanding social therapeutic practice.
All societies are *in* history, even though our typical experience

(both conscious and unconscious) is of living only in society. For, a feature of the society we live in — U.S. society — is that it adapts people to society in a radically ahistorical fashion. Indeed, this adaptation to society is so complete that people often do not even have an awareness that they *are* in history, that history is something it is possible to adapt *to*. In our view, this deprivation of a sense of oneself as historical is a major cause of all varieties of psychopathology. The social therapeutic process helps people to adapt to history, or develop an historical identity. Historical identity is "a synthesis of the personal and the political grounded in the continuous activity of reorganizing one's wants, needs and desires in a collective context toward a collective good, determined collectively" (Holzman & Newman, 1985, p. 65). Helping women of color to redevelop or strengthen their historical identity means empowering them to change the conditions which produce their societal understandings of themselves as "failed superwomen" — a social role in which they cannot survive and grow. In doing so, women of color are then able to become more historical, less societal, and thereby provide leadership to the group and to the community. Thus, women, and in particular women of color, play a key role in the social therapy group. Often they lead in the process of building the groups, which are multi-racial and multi-class, with women and men, gay and straight. They, more than the men, are likely to step out and take emotional risks — to be straight, passionate and compassionate.

THE WOMEN

Susan came into social therapy because of the stresses and strains of her high-powered, corporate job. She earned $50,000 a year, worked for a WASP male corporate executive, and was trying to make herself liked by him. She couldn't understand him or predict his behavior, and was surprised each time he was nasty to her and undermining of her work. Her emotions and reactions to him ran back and forth from anger to obsequiousness. She couldn't understand why he wasn't more supportive of her since she was making so much money for the corporation, or why he wouldn't relate to her as "one person to another." Before entering therapy, she hadn't even considered that her being a Black woman might have something to do with the treatment she was experiencing from her boss. How come being successful wasn't enough to "make up for" being Black? But "making up for" is, in fact, a social practice, not merely a consequence of Susan's success. Her success was contingent upon "making up for" who she historically is, because *being who she is* clearly delimited how far Susan could advance professionally. This woman of color contradiction was well hidden by the social roles of the corporate institution and society generally. The effort to come to terms with the conflict of seeing the problem as her Blackness rather than seeing it as herself pushed Susan out of her narrow, societally determined *individual* identity into what we call a social identity, making it possible for her to work smarter and anticipate her supervisor's responses. Social identity is a learned, cognitive understanding of the social (as opposed to psychological, intrapsychic, or individual) origins of what it means to be a Black woman in this society, of racism, sexism, and classism. Susan's denial that being a Black woman mattered in her day to day dealings at the office was adaptive to the corporate institution's needs, but not at all helpful to Susan either in making life there easier nor in her overall growth.

Susan's *learned* recognition of racism was important, but after all, many people know about racism. Knowing about racism would not translate into making her corporation more accepting of Black people or changing its priorities, but it did give Susan the opportunity to struggle more successfully with what it means to live and grow in this society, rather than merely to mindlessly adapt. Learned recognition of the social contradictions faced by a woman of color in this society is, however, still a far cry from changing the social, emotional, historical conditions which produce the problem in the first place. Historical identity is a critical next step, a qualitative leap.

How is historical identity for women of color produced in the social therapy group? How do women of color help to build community? How do women of color use our history? Answer: We become leaders! This process of developing as leader (actively changing old conditions and producing new ones) is central to the development of one's historical identity. Poor and working class women of color are typically key in this process.

One of the ways in which institutions in this society rob poor women of their history, their culture, their community, their dignity is by stripping them of their right to react to things as they feel and think. As a result, they become increasingly alienated from their emotions and are quick to cover humiliation and shame with anger, drugs and/or depression. In social therapy groups, we work to help poor women of color identify and express their emotional reactions to other people, to racism and to abuse, and help them to expose the humiliation they feel. It is very hard to do this after years of hiding feelings and opinions from welfare workers, school officials, landlords and men who serve as meal tickets. To do so involves creating a community where it can be done. This involves the growth of the social therapy group as the core of such a community, and creating this community greatly enhances the women's ability to provide leadership to the group and to take risks. Which comes first, the chicken or the egg? The community or the leadership? Neither. For the building of the community and the development of leadership are historically inseparable. The group, in turn, extends the practice of social therapy beyond the therapeutic group in coming to depend on and form more intimate relationships with other women of color in the broader therapeutic/political community. Doing so—we can all appreciate—raises many conflicts, and the engagement of them by the therapy group makes it possible for poor women to take steps to actually change the conditions of their lives. Why? Because they have been empowered by history. Their degraded and failed societal identity has begun to give way to their powerful historical identity. They are being validated for the powerfulness of their historic roles rather than vilified for the failure of their societal roles.

We are talking here of the lives of the poor, characterized by devastating and demoralizing instability and crisis. Many of the women share similar histories. Many, although not all, were victims of teen pregnancies often through abusive situations (e.g., sex with older men) that have never been identified as such.

I remember groups where poor women of color began to share the initial sexual experiences of their lives at twelve, thirteen and fourteen with men of twenty, thirty and forty—experiences they never saw as situations where they were being taken advantage of, but instead identified as voluntary, just something in the past that was an expression of their "uncleanliness" and "badness," and, moreover, things they were supposed to be able to cope with. Most of my patients have never spoken of these experiences with anyone else and often aren't aware of the toll the pejorative label "pregnant teen" has on their current life.

Edith had a baby at age fourteen by John, her fifteen-year-old boyfriend for close to a year. Both Edith and John grew up in a rural section of New Jersey in very poor families. Edith's mother took Edith's pregnancy in stride. John disappeared sometime during the early months of the pregnancy and Edith ignored the fact that she was pregnant, hating every moment of it. She eventually had the baby, gave her over to her family and escaped to another city where she constantly was obsessed with her "failure" to be a good mother (a societal failure), and for the next three years suffered through a nervous breakdown.

Joan had her first child at seventeen. Sex was always something that she identified as dirty, and her conception was related to as a punishment for being nasty and fresh. Sex usually took the form of pleasing her boyfriend; it was not then and still is not, fifteen years later, pleasurable. Sex, she says, is something that you do to please men.

Carmen was raped at twelve by an upstanding man in the community. He had been extremely kind to Carmen, and one afternoon she accompanied him to a hotel. When she realized what he really had in mind she said no; he raped her. Her mother knew the circumstances but decided not to do anything about it, not even talking to Carmen. Carmen then signed herself into a home for teenage mothers, gave birth to her son and today has a very abusive relationship with him. He abuses her, and the family understands that to be because Carmen at thirteen was not a good mother and therefore deserves the abuse.

These women enter therapy with descriptions of themselves and understandings of their problems which are stereotypically racist and classist. Part of the ongoing struggle in the context of the social therapy group is to boldly challenge their "sense of self," or individual or societally overdetermined identity. One would think that people would be eager to give up this degraded sense of self, but often they are not, because part of what this would mean for these women is to come to terms with the fact that they, their children and their families are poor and that this is a social historical fact rather than a personal flaw.

Some of the poor women who are in therapy at the Community Clinics of the ISTR have drug and alcohol problems. Some don't. All of them are filled with guilt and self-blame associated with some "mistake" in their lives and the identification of this mistake as the reason for the ongoing psychological and economic crises that is their daily experience; if the mistake had not happened, they would not be poor. Many poor women identify the poverty of their lives as their own fault. Teen pregnancy is often related to as the mistake, the place in life where they went wrong.

Other issues that emerge in the treatment of poor women of color that are essential in the building of the social therapy group have to do with motherhood. Their guilt regarding their children often gets expressed in how they attempt to protect their children from poverty or spend their lives trying to make up to them for its existence. Again, poverty is understood not as a failure of this society to create opportunities for all of its members to live worthwhile lives, but as a personal affliction. Many poor women at some point have been forced to make use of the foster care system or fallen under the scrutiny of the Bureau of Child Welfare; more often than not, this has resulted in their being labelled unfit and/or abusive. The destructiveness of such labels is twofold: the social stigma of being identified as unfit; and second, the absence of support provided to the mother. The label in no way enhances the likelihood of positively changing the relationship between mothers and their children. If anything, it increases the shame, humiliation and anger that these mothers experience. The therapeutic work has identified the syndrome of shame, blame and abuse, and work is done to engage both the tendency of these women to "make up" to their children for being poor and unfit and the abuse that their children heap upon their mothers beginning at very early ages. It serves as a way for the young people to cover up and to not come to terms with who they are and the constraints and limitations in their lives because of the class and races that they have been born into. Their overwhelming message to their mothers is, "You owe me." It is also another way in which new generations are taught sexism that is pervasive in this society.

The "coming out into history" of women of color is extraordinarily empowering. For it is, in actuality, a *return* from societal degradation to cultural/historical pride and power for women of color. This process empowers all who have contributed to the activity of building the environment in which historical energy is released. These very remarks are a product of these women of color. This paper is dedicated to them. Its strength belongs to them. Its inadequacies are due to the societal academic institutions which trained me! For I am one poor woman of color who takes no blame.

REFERENCE

Holzman, L. & Newman, F. (1985). History as an anti-paradigm. *Practice: The Journal of Politics, Economics, Psychology, Sociology and Culture, 3*(3), 60-72.